URBAN TRAILS

SAN DIEGO

URBAN TRAILS

SAN DIEGO

City Parks · Beaches & Bays
Mountains & Canyons

CHRIS GRIFFITH & SUSIE KARA SLATER

MOUNTAINEERS
BOOKS

For Mindy Elkin

I will carry your spirit with me on all my adventures. —Chris

And for Callie Nobriga Pray

Gone too soon, but forever a part of the trail. —Susie

MOUNTAINEERS BOOKS is dedicated to the exploration, preservation, and enjoyment of outdoor and wilderness areas.

1001 SW Klickitat Way, Suite 201, Seattle, WA 98134
800-553-4453, www.mountaineersbooks.org

Printed in China
First edition, 2026

Design and layout: Christina Speed
Cartographer: Mike Powers
All photographs by the author unless credited otherwise
Cover photograph: *Cabrillo National Monument has stunning Pacific vistas (Trail 8).*
Frontispiece: *Moreton Bay fig tree in Balboa Park's Central Mesa (Trail 23)*

Library of Congress Cataloging-in-Publication Data on file for this title.

Mountaineers Books titles may be purchased for corporate, educational, or other promotional sales, and our authors are available for a wide range of events. For information on special discounts or booking an author, contact our customer service at 800-553-4453 or mbooks@mountaineersbooks.org.

Printed on FSC®-certified materials

MIX
Paper | Supporting responsible forestry
FSC® C188448
www.fsc.org

ISBN (paperback): 978-1-68051-796-5
ISBN (ebook): 978-1-68051-797-2

An independent nonprofit publisher since 1960

CONTENTS

BEACHES AND BAYS

NORTH

CENTRAL

MISSION TRAILS

EAST

Colorful flagstone tile in the Spanish Village Art Center (Trail 23)

SOUTH BAY

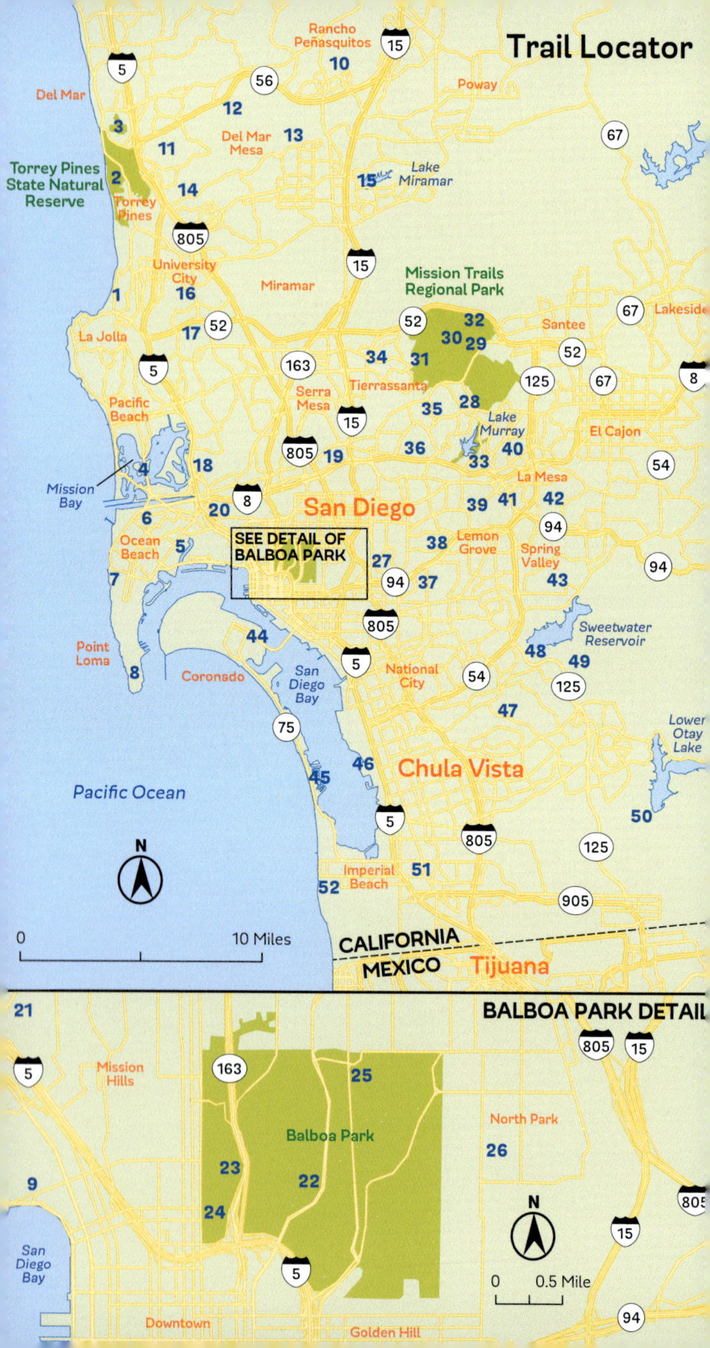
Trail Locator
Rancho Peñasquitos
Del Mar
Torrey Pines State Natural Reserve
Torrey Pines
Del Mar Mesa
Poway
Lake Miramar
University City
Miramar
Mission Trails Regional Park
La Jolla
Santee
Lakeside
Pacific Beach
Serra Mesa
Tierrasanta
Lake Murray
El Cajon
Mission Bay
La Mesa
San Diego
Ocean Beach
SEE DETAIL OF BALBOA PARK
Lemon Grove
Spring Valley
Sweetwater Reservoir
Point Loma
Coronado
San Diego Bay
National City
Lower Otay Lake
Chula Vista
Pacific Ocean
Imperial Beach
0
10 Miles
CALIFORNIA
MEXICO
Tijuana
BALBOA PARK DETAIL
Mission Hills
Balboa Park
North Park
San Diego Bay
0
0.5 Mile
Downtown
Golden Hill

TRAILS AT A GLANCE

Trail	Distance	Walk	Hike	Run	Bike	Kids	Dogs
BEACHES AND BAYS							
1. La Jolla Shores, Coast Walk, and Cove	4.1 miles	•		•		•	•
2. Torrey Pines State Natural Reserve	5.5 miles		•	•		•	
3. Torrey Pines State Natural Reserve Extension	3.3 miles		•			•	
4. Sail Bay	5 miles	•		•	•	•	•
5. Liberty Station to Spanish Landing	4.5 miles	•		•	•	•	•
6. Famosa Slough	2 miles	•		•		•	•
7. Sunset Cliffs Natural Park	4 miles	•	•	•		•	•
8. Cabrillo National Monument	4.7 miles		•			•	
9. The Embarcadero	5.5 miles	•		•	•	•	•
NORTH							
10. Black Mountain	4.1 miles		•	•			•
11. Carmel Mountain Preserve	3 miles		•	•	•	•	•
12. Del Mar Mesa Preserve	4.4 miles	•		•	•	•	•
13. Los Peñasquitos Canyon Preserve	6 miles	•	•	•	•	•	•
14. Lopez Canyon	4 miles		•	•	•	•	•
15. Lake Miramar	4.9 miles	•		•	•	•	•

Trail	Distance	Walk	Hike	Run	Bike	Kids	Dogs
CENTRAL							
16. Rose Canyon	5.3 miles		•	•	•	•	•
17. Marian Bear Memorial Park	6.1 miles		•	•	•	•	•
18. Tecolote Canyon	6.4 miles		•	•	•	•	•
19. San Diego River Trail	1.9 miles	•		•	•	•	•
20. Presidio Park Loop	1.7 miles		•	•		•	•
21. Mission Hills Loop	3 miles	•	•	•		•	•
22. Seven Bridges	5.7 miles	•		•	•	•	•
23. Balboa Park: Central Mesa	2.5 miles	•		•		•	•
24. Balboa Park: West Mesa	3.6 miles		•	•	•	•	•
25. Florida Canyon	3 miles		•	•	•	•	•
26. Switzer and Juniper Canyons	1.8 miles		•	•	•	•	•
27. City Heights Canyons Loop	3.8 miles		•	•		•	•
MISSION TRAILS							
28. Cowles Mountain and Pyles Peak	5.8 miles		•	•			•
29. Kwaay Paay Peak	2.9 miles		•				•
30. North Fortuna	4.4 miles		•				•
31. South Fortuna	4.8 miles		•				•
32. Grasslands Loop	2.5 miles	•	•	•	•	•	•
33. Lake Murray	5.6 miles	•		•	•	•	•
EAST							
34. Shepherd Canyon Loop	3.5 miles		•	•	•	•	•

Trail	Distance	Walk	Hike	Run	Bike	Kids	Dogs
35. Rancho Mission Canyon	3 miles		•	•	•	•	•
36. Navajo Canyon	2.5 miles		•	•	•	•	•
37. Emerald Hills Canyon	3 miles		•	•	•	•	•
38. Chollas Lake	2.3 miles	•	•	•	•	•	•
39. Rolando Village Catwalks	2.4 miles	•		•		•	•
40. The Stride: La Mesa Urban Trail	5.2 miles	•		•	•	•	•
41. La Mesa Secret Stairs	1.5 miles	•		•		•	•
42. Mount Helix	1.7 miles		•	•	•	•	•
43. Dictionary Hill	2.2 miles		•	•	•	•	•
SOUTH BAY							
44. Coronado Walkabout	5.7 miles	•		•	•	•	•
45. Silver Strand State Beach	3.1 miles	•		•		•	
46. Living Coast Discovery Center Trail	1 mile	•				•	
47. Rice and Snake Canyons Loop	4.3 miles		•	•	•	•	•
48. Sweetwater River Trail	3.7 miles		•	•	•	•	•
49. Mother Miguel Mountain	4.5 miles		•	•			•
50. Otay Lakes Loop	1.5 miles		•	•		•	•
51. Otay River Valley Trail	4.7 miles	•	•	•	•	•	•
52. Tijuana Estuary	4.3 miles	•	•	•	•	•	•

Hikers explore the lush tropical oasis that is Palm Canyon (Trail 23).

INTRODUCTION

TRAILS FOR FUN AND FITNESS IN YOUR BIG BACKYARD

SAN DIEGO IS BEST KNOWN for its ideal climate, beautiful beaches, and world-class attractions. "America's Finest City" is massive both by population and acreage. The eighth-largest city in the United States, it boasts a population of 1.4 million people and extends nearly 40 miles from north to south over 342 square miles. San Diego has fantastic weather; its climate is mild and sunny year-round, and the little precipitation it receives comes mostly during the winter. Because of its blue skies, mild temperatures, and large number of park spaces and recreational venues, most residents and visitors enjoy spending time outdoors on the beach, hiking trails, and bike paths.

The topography of San Diego is unique, with mountains in the east giving way to broad mesas intersected by canyons and wide valleys that eventually lead to the ocean. Thanks to these deep canyons and hills separating the mesas, there are small pockets of natural open space scattered throughout the city that give it a hilly geography. San Diego is home to 93 miles of shoreline, including bays, lagoons, and the Pacific Ocean. It contains such a wide range of landscapes, natural features, plants, birds, reptiles, and mammals that even locals are wowed by its diversity.

Urban Trails: San Diego focuses on fifty-two unique routes—one for each week of the year—within the parks and preserves of the metropolitan area. Geographically speaking, the trails are divided into six categories: Beaches and Bays; North; Central; Mission Trails; East; and South Bay. You will find trails to canyons, sandstone bluffs, estuaries, river valleys, beaches, wetlands, lakes, mountaintops, scenic vistas, grasslands, historic sites, vibrant urban communities, and hidden gems. Beaches and Bays focuses on waterfront trails in La Jolla, Mission Bay, Point Loma, and downtown San Diego. North stretches up from State Route 52, covering mountains, mesas, canyons, and lakes in Carmel Valley, Mira Mesa, and Rancho Peñasquitos. Central focuses on the city core of San Diego, highlighting urban canyons, the San Diego River, the Presidio, and Balboa Park. Mission Trails covers the largest city park in San Diego, with 65 miles of paths and five mountain peaks. East explores inland areas east of Interstate 15, including canyons, lakes, mountain peaks, and urban walkways in Southeast San Diego, La Mesa, Rolando Village, Spring Valley, Del Cerro, Allied Gardens, and Tierrasanta. South Bay highlights waterfront trails south of downtown in Coronado, the Silver Strand, Imperial Beach, and Chula Vista, as well as the broad valleys, rivers, lakes and ponds, canyons, and mountain peaks that spread inland from the shores of San Diego Bay.

While many people equate hiking with trails in wilderness or forests, there are plenty of accessible trails at the core of San Diego's urban center. The routes will show you where you can go out for a walk, run, hike, or ride right in your own backyard. These quick outdoor getaways to parks and trails can be done almost anytime, including before or after work or during lunch. Use the book to find routes appropriate for hikers of all ages, skill levels, and ambitions, as well as routes that are perfect for dogs and families.

Expansive ocean views and striking cliff formations along Sunset Cliffs Natural Park (Trail 7)

This guide promotes the parks, preserves, and trails that exist within urban San Diego. The County of San Diego is the most biologically rich county in the continental United States, containing unique and threatened ecosystems that need to be protected. It is important to promote the preservation of natural areas and develop more trails and greenbelts where people live. Urban trails help us reduce our carbon footprint by giving us access to outdoor recreation that is a close drive away or accessible by public transportation or on foot.

So whether you are a visitor or a resident of San Diego, there is something in this book for you. Our goal is to help you develop a new appreciation for the city and add fitness into your routine, based on time spent in nature. Adventure is out there, and it is closer than you imagine. We challenge you to get out there and find it.

In spring, Mission Hills Canyon Trail is green and bursting with wildflowers (Trail 21).

PERMITS, REGULATIONS, AND PARK FEES

Most of the trails described in this book are managed by the various cities or the County of San Diego Parks and Recreation Department. All but a few are free and do not require a permit or fee, but if a trail requires one, we will note it. Regulations such as restricted hours and closures for certain occasions are indicated in each trail's information block.

TRAIL CONDITIONS

In general, these trails change little from year to year, but a rainstorm can wash out bridges or cause other damage to the trails. After any significant weather event, it is best to check with the managing agency to see if a temporary closure is in place.

TRAIL ETIQUETTE

As users of these trails, parks, and preserves, we have an obligation and a responsibility to both respect and preserve them. The educational, nonpartisan, nonprofit organization Leave No Trace Center for Outdoor Ethics (lnt.org) was created for this purpose. Their programs help educate fellow outdoor users about their impact on the environment and recommend techniques to prevent or reduce them. Although the LNT principles are focused more on backcountry hiking and camping, the same concepts still apply to our urban adventures. Keep these important ethics in mind whenever you're outdoors, whether in a park or on a mountain trail:

Pack it in, pack it out. If you take snacks or a picnic lunch to enjoy along your hike, please collect all your waste items to dispose of properly—including apple cores and orange or banana peels. Many trailheads provide waste and recycling containers. Consider carrying an extra resealable bag in your pack for collecting waste items to dispose of at home.

Avoid disturbing wildlife. Remember to observe birds and other animals from a distance. Resist the urge to move closer to wildlife.

Look, don't take. Follow the motto of "Take only photos, leave only footprints." Leave all natural things, such as plants, flowers, rocks, and historical artifacts, as you find them for others to enjoy.

Stay on trail. Don't cut switchbacks, take shortcuts, or make new trails. Doing this will lead to erosion, unsightly trail degradation, and expensive trail repairs.

Obey the rules. Many trails are closed to certain types of users, including dogs and mountain bikers. Some parks or trails are open only during specific hours or certain seasons.

Keep dogs on leash. Most of the trails listed here do allow for canine companions to join you, but they need to be leashed. Also, make sure you pack out their waste.

Observe the right-of-way. Many of these trails allow for mixed use, and as such, those on the trail need to know who has the "right-of-way." All users must yield to any equestrian users, while cyclists must yield to hikers.

Respect the sounds of nature. While many people might enjoy hiking to some music, it can be disruptive to other users, as well as wildlife. If you want to enjoy your favorite playlist, do so with headphones (but keep the volume low enough to hear the world around you).

THE TEN ESSENTIALS

Most of the trails in this guide can be enjoyed with minimal preparation or special gear, but it is always a wise idea to bring water, sun protection, and a few other supplies, regardless of the length of the hike. You may be familiar with something known as the Ten Essentials. This list of ten items that should be carried by hikers was created by The Mountaineers. We have adapted it to a more urban-focused list:

1. **Navigation.** Download or pick up a map of the area you plan to visit, and know how to read it. A cell phone or GPS unit is also good to have along.
2. **Headlamp.** If your hike runs late and you're caught out after dark, you'll be glad to have a headlamp or flashlight to help find your way back to the trailhead. Don't forget spare batteries.
3. **Sun protection.** This is San Diego and not rainy Portland. Always carry sunscreen, rated at least SPF 30 or better, and sunglasses, and wear sun-protective clothing—even on cloudy and foggy days. If the fog lifts or the clouds break, you'll be glad for the extra protection.
4. **First-aid kit.** At the very least, carry a small kit that contains bandages, blister-prevention supplies, tweezers, pain relievers, and antiseptic. If you have allergies (e.g., pollen or bees), you may also want to carry antihistamine tablets or an EpiPen.

The Rotating House, a unique home on Mount Helix (Trail 42)

5. **Knife.** Carry a small pocketknife or multi-tool.
6. **Fire.** While a source of fire, such as a lighter, is considered essential in backcountry destinations, within the context of this guide, you should never need to start a fire for warmth. In fact, doing so could be quite harmful in light of our region's fire danger.
7. **Shelter.** This piece of equipment can simply be a lightweight emergency blanket or poncho that can double as shelter in the event of injury or an emergency.
8. **Extra food.** Pack along a bag of trail mix, sports bars, or energy snacks for emergency pick-me-ups.

Spectacular sunset at Silver Strand State Beach (Trail 45)

9. **Extra water.** Bring enough water to stay hydrated for the length of the hike. You might consider carrying more than you think you'll need, as many of these urban trails are not shaded, and they are warmer than you might expect. It is also a good idea to have cool water or other drinks waiting for you in a cooler in your car.
10. **Extra clothes.** While the weather in San Diego is generally mild, the fog can roll in, making it chilly and damp. It is always advisable to carry an extra insulating layer (e.g., fleece or sweater).

To this list, we add number 11: identification and money. You should always carry some form of identification, such as your driver's license, as well as either a credit or debit card or a few dollars.

WILDLIFE

San Diego is home to a variety of birds, mammals, and reptiles. Most are completely harmless—ground squirrels, rabbits, lizards, and the like—but it is good to know how to respond to others that are present though not often seen.

SNAKES

Rattlesnakes can be found in all parts of the County of San Diego, including the regions covered in this guide. They are usually as interested in avoiding contact as you are. Rattlesnakes tend to favor temperatures between 75°F–90°F, so this usually means you have a higher likelihood of coming across one from late spring through fall. If you do have an encounter, back away and let it move safely off-trail, or at worst, you can turn around.

TICKS

Ticks are present along our trails. They often live on sage scrub and other plants, where they climb to the tips, awaiting a warm-blooded host (that includes dogs). It is wise to perform a tick check periodically along the trail (depending on the trail's makeup) and upon returning to the trailhead. Wearing pants and long sleeves can help reduce your exposure to ticks.

COYOTES

Coyotes are known to roam various trails throughout San Diego. They are most active at dusk and dawn. Usually they will retreat from you. However, it is wise to keep small children and dogs closer along more rural-like trails.

MOUNTAIN LIONS

While extremely rare, mountain lions venturing down from the foothills and mountains have been spotted in urban San Diego. Most notably, in 2019, a small child was attacked by one in Los Peñasquitos Canyon. Thankfully, his father scared it away and the boy recovered. The lion was later located and killed. Remember these tips if you are in possible regions where an encounter might occur:

- Hike with one or more companions.
- Keep children close at hand.
- Never run from a mountain lion. This may trigger its instinct to attack.

Be strategic about responding. Make yourself "large," face the mountain lion, maintain eye contact with it, shout, blow a whistle, and do not act fearful. Do anything to convince the animal that you are not its prey.

POISON OAK

San Diego is home to a wide variety of flora, including eucalyptus trees, Torrey pines, coastal oaks, and, unfortunately, poison oak. This plant contains an oil known as urushiol, which can cause rashes on the skin, or even blisters. Remember the old saying: "Leaves of three, let it be."

Poison oak leaves turn red later in the season.

To distinguish poison oak from other plants with clusters of three leaves, note that poison oak leaves will have edges that are smooth rather than jagged in appearance. The leaves might be red or green, depending on the season. In the winter, poison oak can lose all its leaves, so we recommend avoiding smooth branches. You are more likely to encounter poison oak in the canyons or along streams. If you think you might have encountered poison oak, wash your clothes (and your pet). However, the oil can linger, so other products might be needed if soap and water don't work.

TRAILHEAD CONCERNS

San Diego trails and parks are generally safe places. However, common sense and vigilance are still suggested. Always let someone know when and where you're going and when you expect to return.

CAR THEFT

At some trailheads, car break-ins tend to be more common. Do not leave anything—especially anything of value—in plain sight in your vehicle while out on the trail. Although that duffel might contain only the clothes you will change into upon your return, a thief might think it contains something of value.

UNSHELTERED RESIDENTS

Some trails in this book have a higher chance of encounters with those who are currently unsheltered. Usually there is no direct cause for concern, but just be aware in case an issue might arise. Hikes in the canyons and Balboa Park are more likely to have these encounters.

HIKING WITH YOUR DOG

Many of the trails in this book allow dogs. However, hiking with your pooch when it's hot out can cause them to overheat quickly, so make sure the forecast isn't too warm. Never take your dog hiking when temperatures could exceed 70 degrees Fahrenheit, and remember that your dog's paws are sensitive. Test the temperature of the ground by touching it with the back of your hand for seven seconds: if it's too hot for your hand, it's too hot for your dog.

Always bring plenty of cold, fresh water for your dog and let them hydrate often. If they are slowing down or panting excessively, it's time to give them a break. And remember to keep your pet on a leash while hiking.

SIGNS OF HEATSTROKE IN DOGS

If any of these signs occur, give your dog water, cool them off, and go to a vet immediately.

- heaving panting and/or a rapid pulse
- glazed eyes
- confusion
- vomiting

Rolando Village Catwalks (Trail 39) is a dog-friendly loop with ramps and stairs.

- acting sluggish
- unsteadiness or staggering gait
- deep-red tongue and gums

Dogs have died from heatstroke just taking a walk in the neighborhood in the middle of the day, so please be careful. Just because you're not overheating, that doesn't mean your dog isn't!

A NOTE ABOUT RESTROOMS

Restrooms found in city, county, and state parks and conservation areas range from clean, well-maintained facilities with flush toilets and handwashing sinks to basic chemical outhouses. Sometimes chemical toilets are provided when flush facilities are closed, but not always. This book mentions whether a trailhead has restrooms available, but we cannot guarantee they will always be in service or in good condition.

Crossing the wooden-trestle Quince Street Bridge (Trail 22)

HOW TO USE THIS GUIDE

THIS EASY-TO-USE GUIDEBOOK provides you with the information you need to get outside and walk, run, hike, or bike around San Diego's urban parks, preserves, and other regions. Every trail and path in this guide was hiked by one or both coauthors to ensure that the information, directions, and advice are accurate and up-to-date.

The featured hikes are grouped around general geographic regions of San Diego to help you find hikes that might be close to where you live or work. We have them sorted by those that are near the coast, Mission Bay, or San Diego Bay (Beaches and Bays); those that are near State Route 56 (North); hikes within the core of San Diego (Central); those located in Mission Trails Regional Park (Mission Trails); trails near Interstate 15 (East); and finally, those in the southern portion of San Diego (South Bay).

TRAIL DETAILS

Each hike features a block of information detailing the following:

Distance: This category provides the length of the trail in miles. We used a GPS device to measure all distances for these hikes, then calculated the mileage with CalTopo mapping software (caltopo.com) and Gaia GPS mapping software (gaiagps.com).

Elevation Gain: Most routes include both ascents and descents, but this statistic gives you an overall picture of how much you'll be climbing for the entire trail. We used a GPS device to measure the elevation gain.

High Point: This is the highest elevation on a given hike.

Difficulty: Hikes in this guide are rated *easy*, *moderate*, or *challenging*. The ratings are based on trail surfaces and conditions, distance, and total elevation gain. Most of them are easy to moderate for the average walker, runner, or hiker. Depending on your level of fitness, however, you may find the trails more or less difficult than described.

Fitness: Each trail mentions whether walkers, runners, or hikers might like the route. We think paved paths might be of more interest to walkers, runners, cyclists, or people with mobility issues. If the trail is rougher or hillier, that route might appeal more to hikers.

Family-friendly: In case you are exploring one of these trails with small children, we note optional stopping points like scenic overlooks, which can be perfect spots for a quick snack or even a turnaround point. However, you will be the best judge of whether the child is capable of completing the given hike.

Dog-friendly: This indicates whether dogs are permitted on the trail and what regulations apply. Remember the Leave No Trace principles and be sure to clean up after your dog.

A flower-framed sunset from Sunset Cliffs (Trail 7)

Bike-friendly: This notes whether bicycles are permitted on the trail and if there are any restrictions. Some trails will only be friendly to traditional road bikes, while others will be more suited for mountain biking.

Amenities: These include restrooms, water stations, benches, picnic tables, interpretive signs, viewpoints, shelters, visitor or learning centers, and more. The availability, condition, or service of urban park restrooms can vary dramatically.

Contact: The organization listed here manages the land the trail passes through. Use this information to learn if any closures or special events might impact access to the trail. See Resources at the back of the book for contact information.

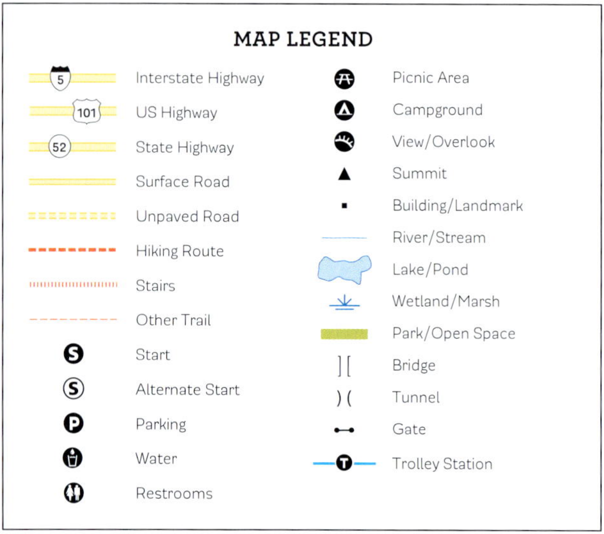

GPS: GPS coordinates for the trailhead (in decimal degrees, north and west values, based on the WGS 84 datum) are provided for each hike.

Before You Go: This optional section includes important information, about details like fees and park hours, to consider while planning and preparing for your outing.

GETTING THERE: Since most people use a smartphone for navigation, under Map to, we have listed the address you should use in your map app to get directions to the trailhead. We have verified that all the addresses work for both Google Maps and Apple Maps. Parking options are listed for each route.

For those wanting to use San Diego's public transit system, we list which route and stop to use to get to the trailhead. Unfortunately, not all trails listed here have convenient public transit stops. Transit options include the San Diego Metropolitan Transit System (MTS) and the North County Transit District (NCTD).

TRAIL HIGHLIGHTS

EACH TRAIL begins with an overview of what you will encounter along its route, including notable landmarks and special features of that area. Highlighting what makes it noteworthy helps you choose among the dozens upon dozens of trails we describe.

GET MOVING: This section provides directions to follow (along with an accompanying map) and the sights that you will see along the way.

GO FARTHER: Look here for ways to extend your hike with additional connecting trails or nearby points of interest.

THE WILD APPEAL OF TORREY PINES

Torrey Pines State Natural Reserve is located within San Diego city limits and yet remains one of the wildest stretches of land on the Southern California coast—a wilderness island surrounded by an urban sea. Due to the efforts and foresight of philanthropist Ellen Browning Scripps, 1500 acres of land remain as they were before San Diego was developed—including maritime chaparral, unspoiled beaches, a lagoon vital to migrating seabirds, and the rarest native pine tree in North America, the Torrey pine (*Pinus torreyana*). Travelers from all over the world visit Torrey Pines, as do local residents who come daily to view overlooks, hike trails, or exercise in a clean, beautiful environment. Torrey Pines has a well-established, popular trail system, including in the main reserve, in the Extension, and along Los Peñasquitos Marsh.

Torrey Pines is open from 7:15 AM to sunset, and there is a parking fee. Trails are generally closed when it rains, to prevent soil erosion. Be aware that Torrey Pines is a reserve, not a park. Of the 279 units in the California State Parks system, only 14 have reserve status; Torrey Pines is one of them. As a reserve, it is a protected conservation area with restrictions not found in parks, such as the following:

- No food or drink, except water, is allowed in the reserve above the beach. Food is fine on the beach (but no alcohol).
- Dogs and pets are prohibited everywhere in the reserve.
- "Pack it in, pack it out" starts from the beach parking lot. Trash and recycling bins are available in the beach parking lots. There are no trash cans in the upper reserve or along the beach.
- Smoking and vaping are prohibited.
- All groups need a permit (some may have to pay a fee).
- Drones are prohibited in the reserve and on the beach.

Retrace your steps back to the staircase, climb the stairs, and follow the trail uphill to a junction with the Broken Hill Trail. Turn right on Broken Hill, the longest trail in the reserve. Make your way uphill through chaparral and sagebrush. At 3.2 miles, turn right at the South Fork Trail junction. Soon after, turn right, following the sign for Broken Hill Overlook.

GUIDE TO COMMON NATIVE FLORA

SAN DIEGO COUNTY IS SAID to be the most botanically diverse county in the continental United States, with more than 2,500 species of wild plants. This guide showcases some of the more prevalent native wildflowers, succulents, trees, and shrubs found within the urban San Diego area. Late winter to spring (February to May) is the best time of year to view San Diego's native plants, when the spring wildflowers bloom and the other plants are green with new growth.

OPPOSITE: *The purple-tinged white flowers of the chaparral yucca*

COMMON NATIVE WILDFLOWERS AND SUCCULENTS

1. California poppy
2. California wildrose
3. Monkeyflower
4. Weed's mariposa lily
5. Showy penstemon
6. Splendid mariposa lily
7. Morning glory
8. Indian paintbrush
9. Sea dahlia
10. Blue-eyed grass
11. Yucca
12. Shaw's agave

COMMON NATIVE SHRUBS AND TREES

1. Lemonade berry
2. Thickleaf yerba santa
3. Manzanita
4. Laurel sumac
5. Toyon
6. Ceanothus
7. Black sage
8. California buckwheat
9. California brittlebush
10. Coast live oak
11. Western sycamore
12. Torrey pine

TRAILS BY TYPE

In addition to referring to the Trails at a Glance chart, use these groupings to select trails suitable for your energy level and/or group on a given outing.

BY DIFFICULTY LEVEL

Easy

Trail 1 La Jolla Shores, Coast Walk, and Cove
Trail 4 Sail Bay
Trail 5 Liberty Station to Spanish Landing
Trail 6 Famosa Slough
Trail 7 Sunset Cliffs Natural Park
Trail 9 The Embarcadero
Trail 11 Carmel Mountain Preserve
Trail 14 Lopez Canyon
Trail 15 Lake Miramar
Trail 19 San Diego River Trail
Trail 20 Presidio Park Loop
Trail 21 Mission Hills Loop
Trail 23 Balboa Park: Central Mesa
Trail 24 Balboa Park: West Mesa
Trail 25 Florida Canyon
Trail 26 Switzer and Juniper Canyons
Trail 32 Grasslands Loop
Trail 34 Shepherd Canyon Loop
Trail 36 Navajo Canyon
Trail 37 Emerald Hills Canyon
Trail 38 Chollas Lake
Trail 39 Rolando Village Catwalks
Trail 44 Coronado Walkabout
Trail 45 Silver Strand State Beach
Trail 46 Living Coast Discovery Center Trail
Trail 51 Otay River Valley Trail
Trail 52 Tijuana Estuary

Moderate

Trail 2 Torrey Pines State Natural Reserve
Trail 3 Torrey Pines State Natural Reserve Extension
Trail 8 Cabrillo National Monument

Trail 12 Del Mar Mesa Preserve
Trail 13 Los Peñasquitos Canyon Preserve
Trail 16 Rose Canyon
Trail 17 Marian Bear Memorial Park
Trail 18 Tecolote Canyon
Trail 22 Seven Bridges
Trail 27 City Heights Canyons Loop
Trail 33 Lake Murray
Trail 35 Rancho Mission Canyon
Trail 40 The Stride: La Mesa Urban Trail
Trail 41 La Mesa Secret Stairs
Trail 42 Mount Helix
Trail 43 Dictionary Hill
Trail 47 Rice and Snake Canyons Loop
Trail 48 Sweetwater River Trail
Trail 52 Otay Lakes Loop

Challenging

Trail 10 Black Mountain
Trail 28 Cowles Mountain and Pyles Peak
Trail 29 Kwaay Paay Peak
Trail 30 North Fortuna
Trail 31 South Fortuna
Trail 49 Mother Miguel Mountain

Steep: Elevation Gain of More than 500 Feet

Trail 2 Torrey Pines State Natural Reserve
Trail 8 Cabrillo National Monument
Trail 10 Black Mountain
Trail 28 Cowles Mountain and Pyles Peak
Trail 29 Kwaay Paay Peak
Trail 30 North Fortuna
Trail 31 South Fortuna
Trail 43 Dictionary Hill
Trail 49 Mother Miguel Mountain

BY DISTANCE

1 to 3 Miles

Trail 6 Famosa Slough
Trail 11 Carmel Mountain Preserve
Trail 19 San Diego River Trail
Trail 20 Presidio Park Loop
Trail 21 Mission Hills Loop
Trail 23 Balboa Park: Central Mesa
Trail 25 Florida Canyon
Trail 26 Switzer and Juniper Canyons
Trail 29 Kwaay Paay Peak
Trail 32 Grasslands Loop
Trail 35 Rancho Mission Canyon
Trail 36 Navajo Canyon

Trail 37 Emerald Hills Canyon
Trail 38 Chollas Lake
Trail 39 Rolando Village Catwalks
Trail 41 La Mesa Secret Stairs
Trail 42 Mount Helix
Trail 43 Dictionary Hill
Trail 46 Living Coast Discovery Center Trail
Trail 50 Otay Lakes Loop

Between 3 and 6 Miles

Trail 1 La Jolla Shores, Coast Walk, and Cove
Trail 2 Torrey Pines State Natural Reserve
Trail 3 Torrey Pines State Natural Reserve Extension
Trail 4 Sail Bay
Trail 5 Liberty Station to Spanish Landing
Trail 7 Sunset Cliffs Natural Park
Trail 8 Cabrillo National Monument
Trail 9 The Embarcadero
Trail 10 Black Mountain
Trail 12 Del Mar Mesa Preserve
Trail 14 Lopez Canyon
Trail 15 Lake Miramar
Trail 16 Rose Canyon
Trail 22 Seven Bridges
Trail 24 Balboa Park: West Mesa
Trail 27 City Heights Canyons Loop
Trail 28 Cowles Mountain and Pyles Peak
Trail 30 North Fortuna
Trail 31 South Fortuna
Trail 33 Lake Murray
Trail 34 Shepherd Canyon Loop
Trail 40 The Stride: La Mesa Urban Trail
Trail 44 Coronado Walkabout
Trail 45 Silver Strand State Beach
Trail 47 Rice and Snake Canyons Loop
Trail 48 Sweetwater River Trail
Trail 49 Mother Miguel Mountain
Trail 51 Otay River Valley Trail
Trail 52 Tijuana Estuary

More than 6 Miles

Trail 13 Los Peñasquitos Canyon Preserve
Trail 17 Marian Bear Memorial Park
Trail 18 Tecolote Canyon

OPPOSITE: *Golden path to the sea on Torrey Pines Extension (Trail 3)*

BEACHES AND BAYS

1 La Jolla Shores, Coast Walk, and Cove

DISTANCE: 4.1 miles roundtrip
ELEVATION GAIN: 430 feet
HIGH POINT: 30 feet
DIFFICULTY: Easy to moderate
FITNESS: Walkers and runners
FAMILY-FRIENDLY: Yes
DOG-FRIENDLY: Yes, leashed. Allowed on beaches, sidewalks, and park areas near beaches 6 PM–9 AM April 1–Oct. 31 and 4 PM–9 AM Nov. 1–March 31.
BIKE-FRIENDLY: Not recommended, due to beach portion
AMENITIES: Restrooms, picnic tables, water, showers, playground, and park areas
CONTACT: City of San Diego
GPS: 32.85740°, –117.25704°
BEFORE YOU GO: Walk at low tide, or at least two or three hours before or after high tide. Popular, so parking areas and pathways may be crowded on weekends and in summer.

GETTING THERE

Map to: 8324 La Vereda, La Jolla, CA 92037

Public Transit: Take MTS Bus Route 30 to La Jolla Shores Drive and Camino del Oro. Walk north on Camino del Oro for 0.1 mile. At El Paseo Grande, follow the paved path through the park to the boardwalk at La Vereda. Turn left and follow the boardwalk 0.1 mile to the lifeguard tower.

Parking: Free parking is available in the large lot at La Jolla Shores.

Are you ready to be wowed by some of the most spectacular coastal views in Southern California? This route links beach walking at La Jolla Shores, sidewalks throughout the La Jolla area, and the short Coast Walk Trail for a total distance of around four miles.

Secluded beach in La Jolla Cove

GET MOVING

Start your hike at the lifeguard tower at La Jolla Shores, a sandy beach that stretches about one mile from the iconic Scripps Pier to The Marine Room restaurant. As you walk south on the beach, gaze out at the ocean where thousands of leopard sharks migrate for their mating season from early June up until October. After about half a mile, you will reach The Marine Room restaurant. Just past the restaurant, turn left through a narrow public coastal access walkway and then turn right once you reach Spindrift Drive.

Follow the sidewalk of Spindrift Drive uphill. At 0.8 mile, turn right on the busy Torrey Pines Road and continue your journey uphill. After about one mile, turn right on Coast Walk and follow the street a short distance to a sign on your right for the historic Coast Walk Trail, sandwiched between rocky cliffs and large homes.

Initially created in 1932, the Coast Walk Trail was given historical significance in 1990. There is evidence, however, that this path is much older—it was used as a Kumeyaay hunting trail up to more than nine thousand years ago. Follow the

A 144-step tunnel leads down to Sunny Jim's Sea Cave.

entrance to the trail, walk over a small parking area, and then pick up the trail again. Cross the white Devil's Slide Footbridge, which was initially constructed in 1931 and rebuilt in 1991. The bridge passes directly above the Rose Canyon earthquake fault line. Continue on the trail, winding along the Pacific Ocean until you reach the Cave Store on Coast Boulevard. Follow the pavement past the Cave Store and then make a right on Coast Boulevard. Take a peek down at Sunny Jim's Sea Cave, which is accessed via a 144-step tunnel at the Cave Store.

When you reach a concrete sign on the right indicating La Jolla Cove 1160 Coast Boulevard, follow the pavement path to the right as it weaves through the La Jolla Cove area toward the Children's Pool. The waters surrounding the cove are part of the 6000-acre San Diego-La Jolla Underwater Park Ecological Reserve. You have ample opportunity to spot wildlife, such as seals, barracuda, opaleye, giant sea bass, baitfish, and orange garibaldi. A little over two miles into your journey, reach the lifeguard station at the Children's Pool, a small beach protected by a seawall. Spend some time here at a popular viewing area for harbor seals. The beach is closed to public access from December 15 to May 15 for harbor seal pupping season. When you are ready, turn around and retrace your path back to the starting point.

GO FARTHER

From La Jolla Shores, head north along the beach past Scripps Pier toward Torrey Pines State Beach. During low tide, you can walk an additional 5 miles to the entrance of Torrey Pines State Natural Reserve. You can also continue your walk through La Jolla on the sidewalk bordering Coast Boulevard past the Children's Pool.

2 Torrey Pines State Natural Reserve

DISTANCE: 5.5 miles roundtrip
ELEVATION GAIN: 700 feet
HIGH POINT: 400 feet
DIFFICULTY: Moderate
FITNESS: Hikers and runners
FAMILY-FRIENDLY: Yes
DOG-FRIENDLY: No
BIKE-FRIENDLY: No; allowed only on Reserve Rd. (Old Highway 1) in uphill direction
AMENITIES: Restrooms, visitor center, benches, and water
CONTACT: California State Parks
GPS: 32.92911°, −117.25977°
BEFORE YOU GO: Most trails are indicated by metal wire fencing. Do this hike during low tide to explore Flat Rock.

High, broken cliffs and deep ravines overlook the ocean at Torrey Pines.

GETTING THERE

Map to: Torrey Pines South Beach, South Beach Lot, 12600 N. Torrey Pines Rd., La Jolla, CA 92037

Public Transit: Take NCTD Bus Route 101 to North Torrey Pines Road and State Beach Reserve. The entrance to the reserve is immediately south, to the right.

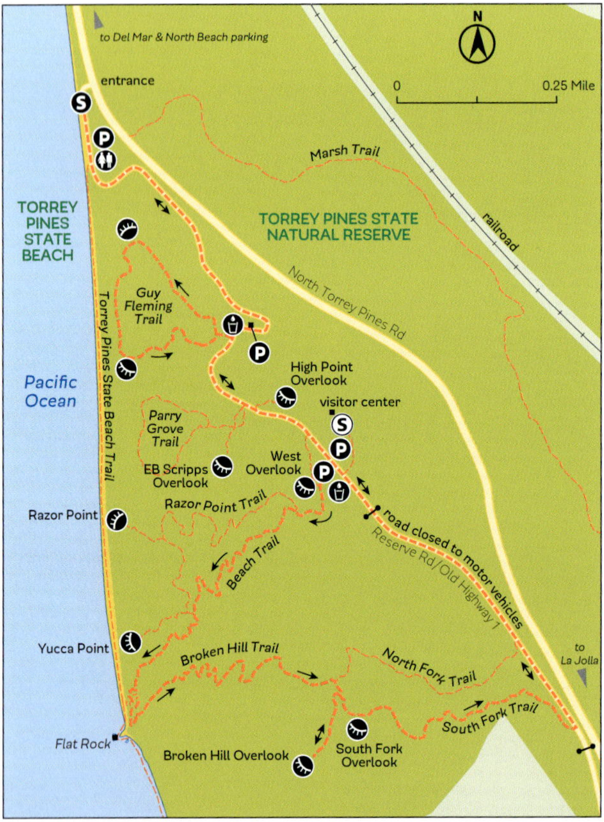

Parking: On North Torrey Pines Road, find free street parking on the west side of the street along Torrey Pines State Beach prior to the entrance. Three main paid parking areas are available: South Beach (at the start of the route described here), North Beach (remote to hiking trails), and Upper Lots (best for touring overlooks and shorter, less strenuous hikes).

Torrey Pines State Natural Reserve is San Diego hiking at its finest. Its fragile environment of high, broken cliffs and deep ravines overlooking the ocean is home to North America's rarest and most geographically restricted type of pine tree species, *Pinus torreyana*. Torrey Pines offers something for everyone—from easy, family-friendly paths to more advanced trails. This moderate 5.5-mile route combines several trails as it travels through the reserve.

GET MOVING

Begin your journey at the reserve's entrance on North Torrey Pines Road at the sign indicating Torrey Pines State Reserve South Beach. Head south, following the paved Reserve Road (Old Highway 1), which is used not only as a vehicular route up to the Beach Trail parking lot, but also as a pedestrian and bicycle pathway. Stay in the areas designated for pedestrians on the shoulder of the road. Climb uphill until you reach the Guy Fleming Trail.

Turn right to follow this 0.7-mile loop through relatively flat terrain. The trail has the greatest variety of wildflowers, ferns, cacti, and habitats in the reserve. Particularly in the spring, look out for heliotrope (*Phacelia distans*), sea dahlia (*Leptosyne maritima*), popcorn flower (*Cryptantha intermedia*), San Diego jewelflower (*Caulanthus heterophyllus*), and a coastal version of California poppy (*Eschscholzia californica*). You will notice two spur trails down to overlooks with vistas of the ocean. Feel free to take in the panoramic views before returning to the trail and continuing onward. Complete the loop and turn right onto the shoulder of Reserve Road.

Walk uphill to the parking lot for the Beach Trail, at 1.7 miles. Turn right into the parking lot and look for the ranger kiosk. Follow the sign for the Beach Trail and begin the 0.7-mile downhill trek to the beach. Keep in mind that this section of trail involves more than one hundred stairs and uneven, sandy terrain. At 2.4 miles, follow the steep staircase down to the rocky beach. If the tide allows, turn left and walk along the beach a short distance to Flat Rock.

The mesmerizing coastal wilderness of pine forests and sandstone canyons at Torrey Pines Extension

Walk 0.1 mile to the spectacular rock formation, which highlights the erosion-shaped geology of the reserve. While the softer Torrey Sandstone has eroded around Broken Hill, a segment capped by the harder Lindavista Formation stands tall. Retrace your steps back to the junction and turn right to rejoin the South Fork Trail.

At around four miles, exit the South Fork Trail and turn left on Reserve Road, which is closed to traffic from here until the parking lot for the Beach Trail. Continue on Reserve Road for 1.5 miles back to the starting point.

GO FARTHER

Add miles exploring the Parry Grove Trail, High Point Trail, Razor Point Trail, and North Fork Trail within the main reserve. If the tide permits, walk along Torrey Pines State Beach. Explore the Los Peñasquitos Marsh Natural Preserve Marsh Trail from the South Beach lot.

3 Torrey Pines State Natural Reserve Extension

DISTANCE:	3.3 miles roundtrip
ELEVATION GAIN:	360 feet
HIGH POINT:	410 feet
DIFFICULTY:	Moderate
FITNESS:	Hikers
FAMILY-FRIENDLY:	Yes
DOG-FRIENDLY:	No
BIKE-FRIENDLY:	No
AMENITIES:	Benches
CONTACT:	California State Parks
GPS:	32.94340°, -117.24871°
BEFORE YOU GO:	Most trails are indicated by metal wire fencing. Some trails are sandy, rocky, or uneven.

GETTING THERE

Map to: 13535 Mira Montana Dr., Del Mar, CA 92014
Public Transit: None
Parking: Follow Mira Montana Drive until the road ends at a cul-de-sac. Free parking is available along the street.

The tiny but mighty Torrey Pines State Natural Reserve Extension lies across Los Peñasquitos Lagoon from the main reserve. The Extension was acquired in 1970, when local conservation groups became concerned with the bulldozing of Torrey pines for residential developments and garnered support from local civic, social, and school groups, as well as national media attention. Unfortunately, a fire struck the the area in June 2024, and at the time of writing, it was being restored.

The Extension has a small network of trails totaling about 3.3 miles, offering a rustic, intimate experience despite being surrounded by housing developments. Hikers will be delighted by

spectacular, dense pine specimens—including half of the three thousand Torrey pines that grow in San Diego—coastal sage scrub and chaparral, eroded sandstone bluffs, and ocean views.

GET MOVING

Begin your hike at the signed entrance peeking out from an opening in a small brick wall. Follow the dirt trail to the left a

Staircase at Torrey Pines Extension

short distance until it meets a paved sidewalk. Continue on the sidewalk as it transitions over a cobblestone road to a dirt path leading to a white gate; this signals the beginning of the Red Ridge Trail. Enter the trail and follow it to the right, passing under the shade of some Torrey pines. After 0.3 mile, come to an open area atop some bluffs. Enjoy the views of the beautifully sculpted sandstone formations, Peñasquitos Lagoon, the main reserve, and the beach. Notice a large log blocking access to the cliffs, your cue to follow the trail left as it turns 180 degrees. At about a half mile into your hike, close the loop and rejoin the trail you came in on. Follow it back to the white gate and retrace your steps back toward the starting point.

At the park's entrance sign, follow the Margaret Fleming Nature Trail to the left, rather than heading right toward the parking area. After about one mile, follow the trail to pass around the left side of a sandstone protrusion. Wind down a series of wooden steps to a canyon. The dry, sandy soils favored by the Torrey pine are also preferred by a variety of other San Diego natives. This coastal sage scrub habitat is rich with wildflowers such as the California poppy (*Eschscholzia californica*) in late winter through early spring, and it supports many sage varieties, including white (*Salvia apiana*), black (*Salvia mellifera*), and coastal (*Artemisia californica*).

Continue hiking until you reach the junction of the Mar Scenic Trail, then turn right. This trail runs alongside and, at times, into the major drainage channel for the Extension. Begin a gentle uphill ascent as you pass through a narrow, eroded channel cut into the dirt.

At 1.6 miles, reach the junction of the Daughters of the American Revolution (DAR) Trail. Turn left here, following signs for DAR Overlook, and continue your climb. After 0.1 mile, turn left at the sign indicating West Ridge DAR Trail. Follow it under the dense canopy of Torrey pines until you reach a wide overlook with wooden benches.

After spending some time taking in the view, loop through the overlook and return to the trail, retracing your steps on the West Ridge DAR Trail back to the junction with the DAR Trail. Turn right to continue on the West Ridge DAR Trail, following the sign for DAR Overlook as you move uphill for 0.1 mile. Make a quick detour to take in the view and plaques at the DAR Overlook before continuing on the West Ridge DAR Trail. Follow it about a quarter mile to reach the junction with the Mar Scenic Trail. Turn right and follow the Mar Scenic Trail 0.2 mile to the junction with the DAR Trail. From this point, retrace your path back to the starting point via the Mar Scenic Trail and Margaret Fleming Nature Trail.

GO FARTHER

Though this route covers most of the trails in the park system, you can add to your hike by completing the out-and-back segment of the DAR Trail.

4 Sail Bay

DISTANCE: 5 miles roundtrip
ELEVATION GAIN: Minimal
HIGH POINT: 60 feet
DIFFICULTY: Easy to moderate
FITNESS: Walkers, runners, and cyclists
FAMILY-FRIENDLY: Yes
DOG-FRIENDLY: Yes, leashed. Allowed on sidewalks and park areas near beaches 6 PM–9 AM April 1 to Oct. 31 and 4 PM–9 AM Nov. 1 to March 31.
BIKE-FRIENDLY: Yes
AMENITIES: Restrooms, picnic tables, water, playgrounds, and park areas
CONTACT: City of San Diego
GPS: 32.76715°, –117.23908°

GETTING THERE

Map to: Sunset Point Park, 1400 Dana Landing Rd., San Diego, CA 92109

Public Transit: Take MTS Bus Route 8 to West Mission Bay Drive and Dana Landing Road. Turn onto Dana Landing Road and follow it west 0.1 mile to Sunset Point Park.

Parking: From West Mission Bay Drive, turn onto Dana Landing Road and follow it west to Sunset Point Park. Free parking is available in the large lot.

Mission Bay is an artificial saltwater bay south of Pacific Beach, created from wetland, marsh, and saltwater bay habitats. Consisting of 4235 acres of roughly equal parts land and water—with 27 miles of shoreline, 19 miles of sandy beach, and 20 miles of paved trails—it is the largest park of its kind in the country. The paved trails are wide, smooth, and flat, with easy parking and restrooms along the way, making the park ideal for pedestrians, cyclists, and skaters. This 5-mile route uses paved paths, sidewalks, staircases, and three low-profile bridges to circle Sail Bay, the most scenic arm of Mission Bay.

GET MOVING

Begin your journey on the paved path at Sunset Point Park. Follow the sidewalk toward West Mission Bay Drive and after a short distance, climb a wooden staircase to the left. At the top of the stairs, turn right on West Mission Bay Drive and walk across the bridge. Though the road is busy, take advantage of the unique perspective it offers, looking down on the bay and its boats and birds as you cross over the water. Mission Bay Park is home to many rare and endangered plant, animal, and bird species—including the California least tern and the light-footed Ridgway's rail.

After about a half mile on the sidewalk, enter the neighborhood of Mission Beach. You will be able to make out the Giant Dipper roller coaster at Belmont Park to the left and the Pacific Ocean straight ahead. At 0.8 mile, turn right on Bayside Walk, a paved trail following the shore of Mission Bay. Continue walking between beach cottages to the left and the sandy shores of Mission Bay to the right. This section is close to the Old Mission Beach business district and restaurants, if you would like to shop or have a bite to eat. After 2 miles, pass the Catamaran Resort and follow the path as it curves to the right and over the Butterfield Cove Bridge, spanning a small tidal channel.

Now in Pacific Beach, you will notice that taller condominiums dominate the left side of the path. Pass Fanuel Street Park and reach the Ingraham Street Bridge at 3.7 miles. Take the staircase to the left instead of continuing along the path.

The bridge near the start of the hike offers an excellent overlook of Sail Bay and Sunset Point Park.

At the top, turn right on Ingraham Street and follow the sidewalk over the bridge to Vacation Isle. Use the crosswalk to head straight through the intersection of Ingraham Street and Vacation Road. Pass over another bridge, catching glimpses of Fiesta Island and SeaWorld to the left.

At the intersection of Ingraham Street and Dana Landing Road, turn right on Dana Landing and follow it to the left along Dana Landing Marina. Cross through the parking lot toward the shoreline. When you reach the boat launch, you will notice a restroom on the left. Continue on the paved path here as it travels between The Dana Hotel on the left and the marina on the right, leading you back to the start at Sunset Point Park.

GO FARTHER

There are nearly 20 miles of paths within Mission Bay Park, including Fiesta Island and the busier Ocean Front Walk running between Pacific and Mission Beaches. This area is an open canvas for all sorts of distances and loops.

5 Liberty Station to Spanish Landing

DISTANCE:	4.5 miles roundtrip
ELEVATION GAIN:	60 feet
HIGH POINT:	30 feet
DIFFICULTY:	Easy to moderate
FITNESS:	Walkers, runners, and cyclists
FAMILY-FRIENDLY:	Yes
DOG-FRIENDLY:	Yes, leashed
BIKE-FRIENDLY:	Yes
AMENITIES:	Restrooms, picnic tables, water, and playground
CONTACT:	City of San Diego, Port of San Diego
GPS:	32.74022°, –117.20925°

GETTING THERE

Map to: 2877 Historic Decatur Rd., San Diego, CA 92106

Public Transit: Take MTS Bus Route 28 to Rosecrans Street and Lytton Street. Walk south 0.2 mile on Lytton Street. Just past the intersection with Truxtun Road, turn right onto the paved footpath entering Liberty Station. Follow this path 0.2 mile to the Liberty Station boat ramp.

Parking: From Rosecrans Street, turn left onto Lytton Street and then right onto Truxtun Road. Turn left onto Perry Road and follow it to the parking lot closest to the Liberty Station boat ramp. Find free parking here or in any of the large lots within Liberty Station.

At the base of the Point Loma peninsula, Liberty Station functioned as the Naval Training Center (NTC) San Diego for seventy-four years, until 1997. The National Park Service listed it on the National Register of Historic Places, preserving forty-nine buildings constructed between 1921 and 1949. Now an urban village, Liberty Station plays host to various events like concerts and 5K runs. It is home to an arts district, public

The USS Recruit *is the only fully commissioned ship in the US fleet to never set sail.*

market, restaurants, shops, residential buildings, hotels, recreational offerings, and a park and open space with a network of trails near the water, parallel to the boat channel. This route explores the western portion of San Diego Bay by connecting Liberty Station's waterfront trails to the Spanish Landing Trail, a shared-use path for pedestrians and bicyclists that is separated from vehicles.

GET MOVING

Begin your route at the Liberty Station boat ramp. Follow the sidewalk southwest along the water, admiring the nice views of downtown San Diego and the airport across the channel. When the sidewalk meets Cushing Road, turn left onto the dirt trail. Though this part of NTC (Naval Training Center) Park features several meandering trails, continue on the one that hugs the perimeter of the open space along the water.

After about 0.4 mile, reach the manicured part of NTC Park, featuring large landscaped lawns, playgrounds, picnic tables, and even a rose garden. Here, you can walk on the

Views of the marina and Harbor Island along the Spanish Landing Trail

paved path or the parallel dirt trail. Often you will see people exploring on the water here, as this is a great place to launch a kayak or paddleboard. Continue on the path through NTC Park past several hotels on the right.

At just under one mile, shortly after passing the pedestrian Nimitz Bridge, turn right. Follow the sidewalk a short distance to check out the USS *Recruit*, the only fully commissioned ship in the US fleet to never set sail. This ship is where more than fifty thousand recruits learned the skills to serve aboard other naval warships. Walk around the perimeter and

visit the free exhibition inside, which is open Saturday and Sunday from 12 PM to 4 PM.

Walk back to the Nimitz Bridge and use it to cross over the channel. At the end of the bridge, turn right on the paved path, then turn right on the Spanish Landing Trail and follow it under the vehicular Harbor Bridge. As the trail moves east, take in views of Point Loma and Coronado on the right. Pass through Spanish Landing Park, a California Historical Landmark commemorating the site of the 1769 meeting of the Gaspar de Portolá and Father Junípero Serra expeditions. Spanish Landing Park is home to a small sandy beach, picnic tables, benches, restrooms, playground equipment, and beautiful marina views.

Continue on the Spanish Landing Trail until, at about 2.2 miles, you reach Cancer Survivors Park, funded by Richard and Annette Bloch. Take a loop through the Positive Mental Attitude Walk, where fourteen plaques suggest uplifting lifestyle adjustments and strategies to improve mental health and face life's challenges. This will bring you adjacent to the San Diego International Airport, which is a good place to turn around. Retrace your steps back to the starting point.

GO FARTHER

Continue on past Spanish Landing to the Embarcadero into downtown San Diego, or add on additional miles on Harbor Island.

6 Famosa Slough

DISTANCE: 2 miles roundtrip
ELEVATION GAIN: Minimal
HIGH POINT: 30 feet
DIFFICULTY: Easy
FITNESS: Walkers and runners
FAMILY-FRIENDLY: Yes
DOG-FRIENDLY: Yes, leashed
BIKE-FRIENDLY: Not recommended; path narrow and brushy at times
AMENITIES: Restrooms and benches
CONTACT: City of San Diego
GPS: 32.74806°, –117.22939°
BEFORE YOU GO: There are often unhoused individuals and encampments in this area. While we did not feel unsafe at any point while hiking here, if it makes you uncomfortable, plan to do this one with a buddy or join one of the monthly group nature walks sponsored by the Friends of Famosa Slough.

The 30-acre marshy wetland at Famosa Slough

GETTING THERE

Map to: 2598 Famosa Blvd., San Diego, CA 92107

Public Transit: Take MTS Bus Route 35 to West Point Loma Boulevard and Famosa Boulevard, directly in front of Famosa Slough.

Parking: From Famosa Boulevard, cross Valeta Street and find free parking in the dirt lot at the trailhead.

Famosa Slough is a 37-acre State Marine Conservation Area in Point Loma, managed by the San Diego Parks and Recreation Department with help from Friends of Famosa Slough. It offers a small network of trails on both its 12-acre channel and 25-acre southern portions and protects the fragile habitat near where the San Diego River meets the Pacific Ocean. Famosa Slough was originally part of the Mission Bay wetland complex, but over time, it was gradually separated for various industrial uses, which caused public outrage and a movement to protect the slough. About 95 percent of California's wetlands have been lost to development, and you will notice that the area surrounding this pocket of wetlands is no exception.

GET MOVING

From the dirt parking area, walk north through the yellow posts. Take the trail to the right and follow it along the fence line. You will notice residential buildings on the right—they are a fixture on the perimeter of this route, as they skirt the edge of the slough from all directions. The first part of this route circles the southernmost portion of the park; continue on the trail as it goes around three sediment depressions, with plants growing near and between concrete jacks and interlocking blocks to slow down runoff from the adjacent areas.

At 0.2 mile, nearly back to the parking lot, make a right to turn away from it at the trail junction and follow the bricks uphill, crossing the concrete walkway to Montalvo Street. Turn right on the dirt trail, following it along the fence as it passes through a tree arch and a thriving native plant restoration area with coastal goldenbush, California buckwheat, laurel sumac, California brittlebush, blue elderberry, and broom baccharis. At 0.3 mile, cross Mentone Street and pick up the trail along the west side of the slough.

After about a tenth of a mile, turn right and take the short trail down to a viewpoint. Benches are placed here and throughout the slough at key spots for bird-watching. A popular spot for bird-watchers year-round, the slough is a frequent stopover point for migrating birds in the winter. More than 240 species of birds have been spotted here. Return back to the main trail and turn right to continue onward. At 0.5 mile, turn right and make a detour to another viewpoint.

After circling back to the main trail, turn right and move past the signed kiosk to the intersection of Famosa Boulevard and West Point Loma Boulevard. Turn right on West Point Loma

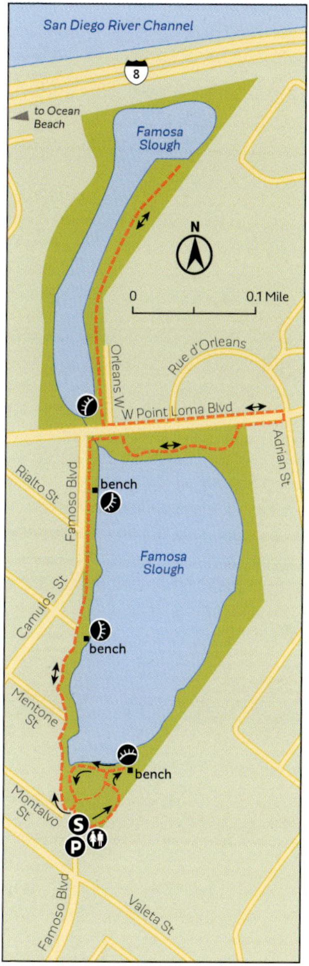

Boulevard and follow the sidewalk for a short distance before turning right onto the wide dirt path. Follow it along the slough as it curves back to West Point Loma Boulevard. Accessing the other portion of Famosa Slough requires crossing the busy West Point Loma Boulevard, so turn right on West Point Loma and walk on the sidewalk until the gas station at the intersection of Adrian Street and West Point Loma.

Use the crosswalk to cross West Point Loma and turn left, then follow the sidewalk west. Turn right on the trail at the signed entrance to Famosa Slough, just past Orleans West. Here, the remnants of a wooden trestle are visible to the left. Follow the trail north toward Interstate 8, with the slough on the left and residential buildings on the right.

The trail eventually peters out at the point where you can see the highway crossing the inlet to the San Diego River Channel. This is a good point to turn around and retrace your steps back to the starting point.

GO FARTHER

Consider extending your trip to the nearby Point Loma Native Plant Garden, a hidden gem featuring many rare and endangered native plant species.

7 Sunset Cliffs Natural Park

DISTANCE: 4 miles roundtrip
ELEVATION GAIN: 120 feet
HIGH POINT: 130 feet
DIFFICULTY: Easy to moderate
FITNESS: Walkers, hikers, and runners
FAMILY-FRIENDLY: Yes; stay away from cliff edges and watch for signs warning of erosion
DOG-FRIENDLY: Leashed dogs allowed on beaches, sidewalks, and park areas near beaches 6 PM–9 AM April 1 to Oct. 31 and 4 PM–9 AM Nov. 1 to March 31
BIKE-FRIENDLY: Yes, except certain trails in cliffside park where signed "No bikes"
AMENITIES: Restrooms and benches
CONTACT: City of San Diego
GPS: 32.73575°, –117.25550°
BEFORE YOU GO: This area is popular with surfers, ocean-gazers, and folks who like to cruise Sunset Cliffs Blvd.

GETTING THERE

Map to: Intersection of Sunset Cliffs Blvd. and Adair St., San Diego, CA 92107

Public Transit: Take MTS Bus Route 923 to Point Loma Avenue and Sunset Cliffs Boulevard. Walk down Point Loma Avenue, cross the street at Sunset Cliffs Boulevard, and turn left to begin the trail.

Parking: Find street parking along Sunset Cliffs Boulevard or Adair Street. There are also several free parking lots along

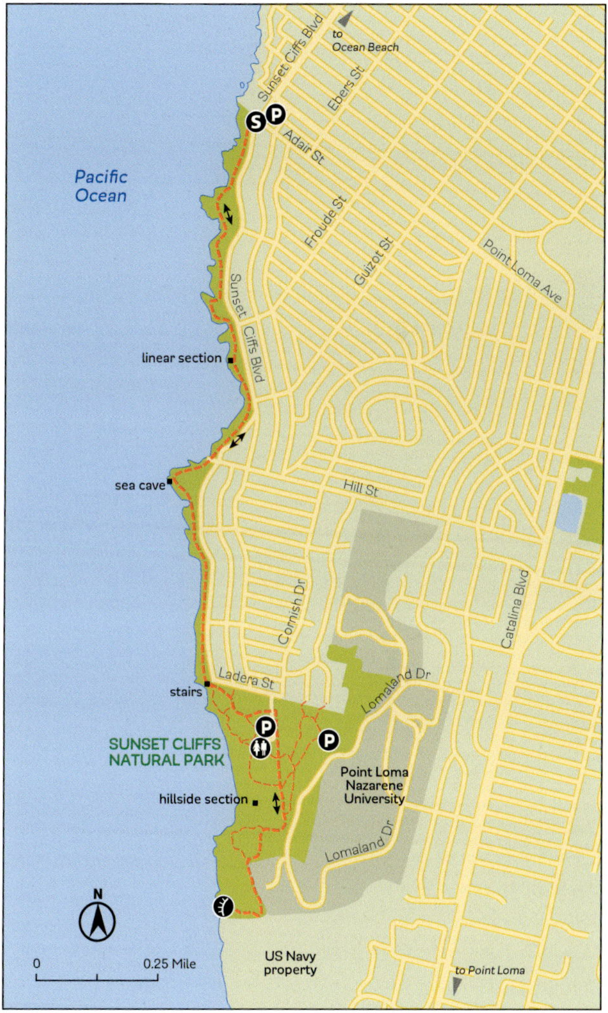

Sunset Cliffs Boulevard, as well as one on Lomaland Drive on the campus of Point Loma Nazarene University, and one on

Sunset Cliffs is one of the best spots in San Diego to catch a sunset.

the corner of Ladera Street and Cornish Drive. Keep in mind that spots are limited and can fill up quickly during the hours around sunset.

This 68-acre coastal park extends 1.5 miles along the Point Loma peninsula's western shoreline, with gorgeous panoramic views of the Pacific Ocean. The park has a linear and a hill-side section with links to the Point Loma Ecological Reserve. Though the City of San Diego dedicated the park in 1983, Sunset Cliffs dates back millions of years. Fossils of mosasaurs from the Late Cretaceous epoch unearthed here are displayed at the Natural History Museum. The area was also inhabited by the Indigenous Kumeyaay Tribe, who believed Sunset Cliffs was sacred land to be shared by all.

This route explores both sections, combining dirt trails and pavement. The unique coastal environment features ocean views, cliff formations and caves, an intertidal area, and a native coastal sage scrub habitat. As its name implies, it is also one of the best places in the County of San Diego to catch a sunset.

GET MOVING

Begin your walk at the signed kiosk near the intersection of Adair Street and Sunset Cliffs Boulevard. In the linear section of the park, follow the hard-packed dirt trail wedged between the street and the cliffs overlooking the ocean. Periodically, you will encounter small parking lots or signs that read "Unstable Cliffs; Stay Back; No Public Access." When this occurs, veer to the left and follow the shoulder of Sunset Cliffs Boulevard. There is a large section of the boulevard where white delineator posts further protect the walking area. As you go, notice the ocean views, beaches, arches, and cliff formations, including a fenced-off open-ceiling sea cave; keep your eyes peeled for California gray whales, often seen migrating annually from the Bering Sea to Baja California and back during winter months.

At 1.3 miles, reach a metal staircase at Ladera Street, providing access to the beach and tide pools below. The best time to head to the beach is at low tide. Immediately following the staircase, there is a sign indicating you have reached the hillside section of the park. Here there is a free-form trail system across a native coastal sage scrub habitat that weaves up and down the hillside and coast. Feel free to explore on your own, or follow the route described below to the southern terminus of the park.

Enter the hillside section. Follow the signs for "trail" and restrooms as you bear left. Continue straight and cross a gravel driveway. Head left (or veer right if you need a pit stop at the parking lot restrooms) and follow the path uphill. Cross

Staircase to the sea at Sunset Cliffs

over the road and continue a short distance uphill until you meet a wide, flat path at 1.5 miles. Turn right and follow the path for about 0.2 mile. At a trail junction with various side trails, continue straight and then veer to the right at the trail marked with a No Bikes sign. Stay right and continue over a wooden bridge. Follow the trail left, then right, uphill toward the fence line, following it toward the ocean until you reach two benches overlooking the water, indicating you have reached the end of the trail after about two miles of walking. Have a seat and soak up the views before you retrace your steps to return to the starting point.

GO FARTHER

In the linear section, you will encounter various spur trails down to the bluffs. In the hillside part, there are additional trails weaving in and out of the cliffs and heading up the hillside toward Point Loma Nazarene University. During extreme negative tides in the winter, it is possible to explore the coastline and sea cave that is encircled in fencing.

8 Cabrillo National Monument

DISTANCE: 4.7 miles roundtrip
ELEVATION GAIN: 750 feet
HIGH POINT: 420 feet
DIFFICULTY: Moderate
FITNESS: Hikers
FAMILY-FRIENDLY: Yes; can be broken up into smaller sections by driving to parking lot on coast
DOG-FRIENDLY: No; leashed dogs allowed only in small portion of park along Coast Trail
BIKE-FRIENDLY: No; allowed on Cabrillo Memorial Dr. but not on trails
AMENITIES: Restrooms, water, visitor center, benches, lighthouse, and military exhibits
CONTACT: National Park Service
GPS: 32.67444°, -117.24049°

Old Point Loma Lighthouse framed by California buckwheat

BEFORE YOU GO: Admission fee. Open daily 9 AM–5 PM. Bayside and Oceanside Trails close at 4 PM and coastal area closes at 4:30 PM. To explore tide pools, do this hike at low tide, or at least two to three hours before or after high tide.

GETTING THERE

Map to: 1800 Cabrillo Memorial Dr., San Diego, CA 92106

Public Transit: Monday through Friday, take MTS Bus Route 84 to Cabrillo National Monument. Begin your route from the bus stop near the visitor center.

Parking: From Catalina Boulevard, go through the Navy gate and follow the road to its end. Pay the fee at the entrance station and continue on Cabrillo Memorial Drive to the parking lot closest to the visitor center. Alternate parking is available in three small lots in the coastal area.

Cabrillo National Monument, at the southernmost end of Point Loma peninsula, is San Diego's only National Park Service property. This tip-of-land perch offers astounding views of San Diego Bay and the Pacific Ocean, plus excellent opportunities to explore the natural, historical, and cultural significance of the area. There is a monument and information about Juan Rodríguez Cabrillo, who in 1542 became the first European explorer to set foot on the West Coast of North America. You can also find the Old Point Loma Lighthouse and military buildings used as part of Southern California's defense system during World War II.

A small network of hiking trails twists through 660 acres of coastal habitat. This route makes it possible to explore the majority of the park on foot.

GET MOVING

Begin at the visitor center, where you can see exhibits, use the restroom, and enjoy views of downtown San Diego and Coronado from the Cabrillo statue. Follow the sidewalk toward the

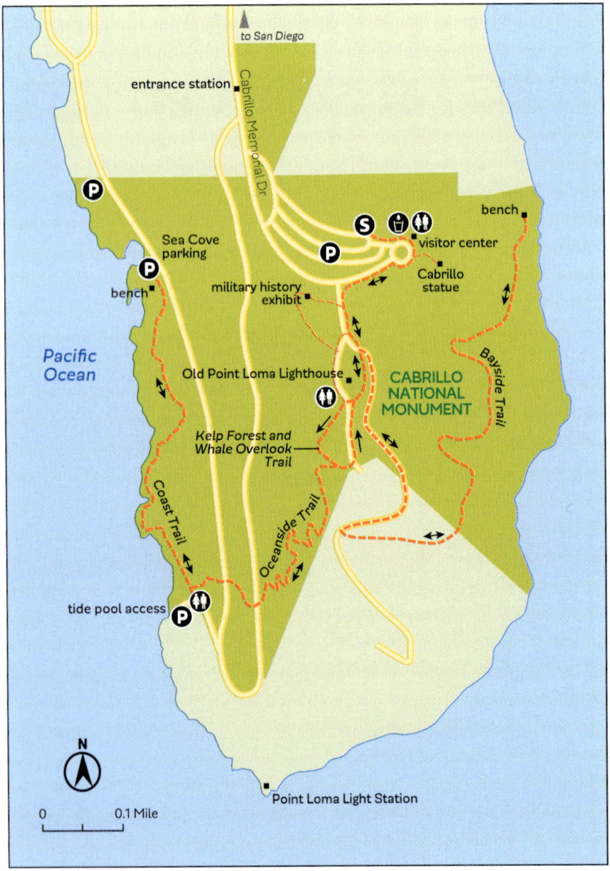

lighthouse, moving uphill as the path veers left. After about a quarter mile, reach the junction with the Bayside Trail to the left. Continue straight, then turn right onto the walkway to the lighthouse, which was built in 1855 and remained in use until 1891, when a newer electric lighthouse, visible from the Oceanside Trail, was constructed on Point Loma's

The Oceanside Trail at Cabrillo National Monument

southernmost tip. Here, you can enter the lighthouse and climb partway up the tower.

Turn right after the lighthouse, then go left onto the walkway overlooking the ocean, and shortly after, turn right on the short Kelp Forest and Whale Overlook Trail, which is wheelchair and stroller accessible. During the winter, watch for migrating gray whales. After 0.1 mile, turn right onto the Oceanside Trail, Cabrillo's newest addition, which opened in April 2024. It connects the upper portion of the park with the coast section. Enjoy views of the Pacific as you head downhill, moving past historical defense structures and through a rare, undeveloped coastal scrub environment with native plants and wildflowers. Watch your footing, as this trail has narrow areas, steps, steep portions, uneven surfaces, and switchbacks. Cross Cabrillo Memorial Drive and regain the trail twice to continue to its end at the information kiosk for the tide pool area at 0.9 mile.

Turn right on the Coast Trail, following the paved path as it transitions to dirt and then taking stairs downhill toward the tide pools. During winter low tides, this is one of the best-preserved rocky intertidal areas open to the public on Southern California's coast. Continue on the Coast Trail as it drifts north along the coast—winding up, down, and along bluffs and over and around eroded sandstone ravines, using staircases. Follow signs for Sea Cove parking, and reach it at 1.4 miles. Take advantage of the bench here to rest and gaze out at the ocean.

Retrace your steps on the Coast and Oceanside Trails back to the Kelp Forest and Whale Overlook Trail, at 2.4 miles. Turn right and follow the path to the signed junction for the Bayside Trail, at 2.5 miles. Take a sharp right on the road and follow it downhill. After 0.3 mile, take a hard left on the gravel trail. Continue on the Bayside Trail as it descends toward San Diego Bay until it dead-ends at US Navy property at 3.5 miles.

Rest on the benches and enjoy views of San Diego, Coronado, the Pacific Ocean, Mexico, and the surrounding mountains to the north and east. Observe sailboats and ships moving through the bay's narrow entrance. When you are ready, turn around and follow the Bayside Trail back to its intersection with the sidewalk. Turn right and follow it downhill back to the visitor center.

GO FARTHER

Catalina Boulevard (Cabrillo Memorial Drive) and the Point Loma Ecological Reserve are accessible to pedestrians and bicycles via the road, but be cautious and aware that there is no sidewalk.

9 The Embarcadero

DISTANCE: 5.5 miles roundtrip
ELEVATION GAIN: Minimal
HIGH POINT: 20 feet
DIFFICULTY: Easy to moderate
FITNESS: Walkers, runners, and cyclists
FAMILY-FRIENDLY: Yes; flat terrain easily accessible to strollers and children
DOG-FRIENDLY: Yes, leashed
BIKE-FRIENDLY: Yes
AMENITIES: Restrooms, picnic tables, benches, water, playground, museums, and food
CONTACT: Port of San Diego
GPS: 32.72753°, –117.17755°
BEFORE YOU GO: Start early for fewer crowds, as this area is very popular. Some portions, usually the Embarcadero Marina Park North and South, can close for special events.

GETTING THERE

Map to: Intersection of W. Laurel St. and N. Harbor Dr., San Diego, CA 92101

Public Transit: Take MTS Bus Route 923 or 992 to North Harbor Drive and Laurel Street.

Parking: From North Harbor Drive, pull into the one-way parking lot near West Laurel Street, running parallel to the Embarcadero and North Harbor Drive, and find a spot. Parking is metered seven days a week here. The Port of San Diego offers twenty free public parking spots on North Harbor Drive between West Hawthorn Street and West Grape Street.

Downtown San Diego's scenic Embarcadero offers a paved walkway that curls along San Diego Bay, one of the world's finest natural deep-water harbors. The 22-square-mile bay is nearly landlocked, sheltered by two overlapping peninsulas—Point Loma and Silver Strand—and connected to the Pacific Ocean by a narrow channel. *Embarcadero* means "the landing place," and the bay is a major international shipping hub, as well as home to one of the country's most extensive military base complexes.

This area is popular with tourists and locals alike, who come to recreate outdoors and experience the Embarcadero's unique blend of history, culture, shopping, and entertainment. You can jog, walk, or bicycle while being treated to beautiful waterfront views. Though there is no set starting point for the Embarcadero, this route explores the majority of the pathway and its parks.

GET MOVING

Begin your journey on the Embarcadero's paved pathway near the intersection of West Laurel Street and North Harbor Drive. Walk south and look out at the bay to your right, where you will see boats and Coronado. This "island" is actually a tied island, meaning it is connected to the mainland in Imperial Beach by a narrow strip of beach, the Silver Strand. This barrier creates a calm bay used not only for commerce, military, and recreation but also as a sanctuary for wildlife. Interpretive panels along this route describe the wildlife you might see, including shorebirds, marine mammals like the harbor seal and sea lion, and mollusks like the California mussel in beds on piers and rocks.

After 0.4 mile, the County of San Diego Administration Center and Waterfront Park, with its interactive 830-foot-long

Up-close views of the San Diego Bay from the Embarcadero

Look for Embracing Peace, *a statue by John Seward Johnson II, in Tuna Harbor Park.*

splash fountain, will appear on your left—a great stop for kids of all ages on warm days. At 0.6 mile, on the right, pass the Maritime Museum and its star attraction, the world's oldest sailing ship still in regular use, the 1863 *Star of India*. Stroll past the Portside Pier, an over-the-water dining complex, and the cruise ship terminal to the right. To the left is Lane Field

Park, once home to the original San Diego Padres stadium more than eight decades ago. Walk past the Broadway Pier before reaching the Navy Pier, where the USS *Midway* aircraft carrier is permanently berthed as a museum.

At 1.2 miles, at the intersection of West G Street, turn right and follow the sidewalk to make a detour through Tuna Harbor Park. Check out art like the *Embracing Peace* statue and the *National Salute to Bob Hope and the Military*, as well as a viewpoint overlooking Naval Air Station North Island. After enjoying the views, return back to the Embarcadero walkway and turn right to continue past Ruocco Park to Seaport Village, a shopping district filled with shops, restaurants, and a carousel with hand-carved animals dating back to 1895.

At 1.8 miles, turn right to follow the looping sidewalk along the Embarcadero Marina Park North Promenade, enjoying 360-degree views of the surrounding area, including the Coronado Bridge. After completing the loop, turn right to rejoin the main Embarcadero path. Walk past the San Diego Convention Center, and for more of a challenge, join local fitness enthusiasts in running its one-hundred-step staircase.

At 2.8 miles, turn right to explore Embarcadero Marina Park South Promenade, home of the Rady Shell at Jacobs Park. If you time your walk right, you will be treated to the sounds of the San Diego Symphony or a famous artist performing a concert. Follow the sidewalk to the right of the concert venue and loop around the park—which includes a parcourse with stations for push-ups, dips, and pull-ups—alongside grass and views for days. Once you complete the loop, turn left and return to the main Embarcadero path. Follow it back to the starting point. Or if you are tired, grab a pedicab!

GO FARTHER

The Embarcadero has connections to the 24-mile Bayshore Bikeway, linking downtown San Diego, National City, Chula Vista, Imperial Beach, the Silver Strand, and Coronado. You can also walk along the Embarcadero past the airport toward Spanish Landing and Liberty Station.

OPPOSITE: *Autumn leaves in Los Peñasquitos Canyon (Trail 13)*

NORTH

10 Black Mountain

DISTANCE:	4.1 miles roundtrip
ELEVATION GAIN:	820 feet
HIGH POINT:	1550 feet
DIFFICULTY:	Challenging
FITNESS:	Hikers and runners
FAMILY-FRIENDLY:	No
DOG-FRIENDLY:	Yes, leashed
BIKE-FRIENDLY:	Yes, but one section may require you to dismount
AMENITIES:	Restrooms and water
CONTACT:	City of San Diego
GPS:	32.97124°, -117.11745°

GETTING THERE

Map to: 9711 Oviedo Way, San Diego, CA 92129

Public Transit: None

Parking: Parking is available at Hilltop Community Park or along Oviedo Way.

Black Mountain and its microwave antenna towers stand out prominently for residents of northern San Diego. This peak is located in the 2352-acre Black Mountain Open Space Park and has several trails to its summit.

GET MOVING

From the parking lot at Hilltop Community Park, locate the Nighthawk trailhead and kiosk at the east end of the lot. Start climbing up the old jeep road to the east, staying to the left at any junctions. After about 0.2 mile, the trail will level off for a while. Go straight, past the two side trails that connect with the road and high school below. The summit will be in view for almost the entire hike as you work your way along the sage- and chaparral-lined trail. The way dips down for a short section, where a trail to the right leads to trails on the eastern

side of Black Mountain Open Space Park. Continue straight to reach the summit, and keep climbing upward.

After about 1.3 miles, the Nighthawk Trail ends at the junction with the Miner's Ridge Connector Trail. Notice the safety signposts that describe your location using the What Three Words method. To learn more about this alternate location method, visit what3words.com. Turn left at this junction and make the rocky, steep, but thankfully relatively short climb to reach the service road. The summit is about 0.7 mile away.

The sage- and chapparal-lined trail at Black Mountain

You will probably start to see more people along this section; most mountain bikers use the service road for their route to the summit, and the service road trailhead is located in a neighborhood, so residents will opt for this route too. Continue past the microwave towers to the north side of the summit, where you will find a couple of benches to rest on and soak in the view, as well as a summit sign.

While you don't get a 360-degree view from any location, you can walk around the summit to take it all in. On a clear day, you should be able to spot San Clemente and Catalina Island to the west and the Coronado Islands off to the south. If conditions are right, you might see paragliders soaring around. Once done taking in the view, return by the same route. If you are here to enjoy a sunset, make sure you bring a headlamp to avoid any rocks along the trail that might lead to a sprained ankle on the way back.

GO FARTHER

As you make your way to the summit, you'll pass several junctions, most notably the trails on the eastern side of the park and the connection to the Miner's Ridge Loop Trail. Both of these options provide several more miles of exploration of Black Mountain Open Space Park.

11 Carmel Mountain Preserve

DISTANCE: 3 miles roundtrip
ELEVATION GAIN: 270 feet
HIGH POINT: 430 feet
DIFFICULTY: Easy
FITNESS: Hikers, runners, and cyclists
FAMILY-FRIENDLY: Yes
DOG-FRIENDLY: Yes, leashed
BIKE-FRIENDLY: Yes
AMENITIES: Restrooms and water
CONTACT: City of San Diego
GPS: 32.92592°, -117.21847°
BEFORE YOU GO: Visit Carmel Mountain Preserve in the late winter or early spring months to see the vernal pools.

GETTING THERE

Map to: Intersection of Fairport Way and Shorepointe Way, San Diego, CA 92130

Public Transit: None

Parking: From Carmel Mountain, turn onto East Ocean Air Drive. Turn left onto Fairport Way. Find free street parking at the trailhead near the intersection of Fairport Way and Shorepointe Way. Additional parking is available in the large lot at the adjacent Ocean Air Community Park and Recreation Center.

The 300-acre Carmel Mountain Preserve is a pocket of nature within the heavily developed Carmel Valley area of San Diego. Offering a trail system for hikers, equestrians, and mountain bikers, it is also part of the San Diego Multiple Species Conservation Plan.

The preserve was established in the late 1990s to protect several sensitive coastal ecosystems after a years-long grassroots campaign to block a residential housing development. Not only does this preserve have scenic red rocks, views of Torrey Pines State Natural Reserve, and ocean sunsets,

A toyon's vibrant winter bloom

but it also boasts southern maritime chaparral, coastal sage scrub, wet meadows, and vernal pools. These unique habitats support more than two dozen rare species, several of which are federally endangered, such as the California gnatcatcher, San Diego fairy shrimp, and Del Mar manzanita.

GET MOVING

From Fairport Way, walk up a short section of the gravel service road to the preserve's gate. Pass through the gate and

Hiking side by side at the Carmel Mountain Preserve

walk uphill less than a tenth of a mile before turning left at the first trail junction. Be careful of your footing, as the trail is covered with small, marble-sized concretions and can be slippery. At 0.25 mile, continue straight through the intersection with the utility line service road. At 0.5 mile, come to a bench and a viewpoint over the Peñasquitos Lagoon and Torrey Pines State Natural Reserve.

Next, look for the continuation of the path to the right of the viewpoint. Watch your step as you make a very steep descent down the sandstone substrate. At 0.7 mile, follow the trail as it curves to the right into a canyon, and at 0.8 mile—at the edge of the grove of eucalyptus trees to your left—follow the narrow singletrack trail as it turns to the right. This section of trail is sandy at times. Make a gradual climb through the southern maritime chaparral, which includes toyon, lemonade berry, laurel sumac, wild cucumber, and black sage. The trail slowly transitions through coastal sage scrub habitat as you move back to the original plateau.

Once you are on the plateau, there are various intersecting trails. The route suggested here generally forms a clockwise loop around the perimeter of the preserve. At 1.2 miles, turn right at the trail junction. Continue straight across the utility road and pick up the trail again on the right. Then, at 1.3 miles, turn left. This portion of the trail contains numerous vernal pools, some of the 3 percent that still remain in California. Many of the pools in this area have been damaged and are being rehabilitated. The trails are mostly lined with cables here to remind users to avoid the pools. On your left, find a wooden viewing platform. After it rains, when there is water in the pools, look closely for tadpoles, fairy shrimp, and plants that are endemic to this ecosystem.

Continue on the trail, and at 1.6 miles, turn left at the junction and move downhill toward the ocean. After a short distance, turn right and then right again at the next trail intersection. Continue straight at 1.8 miles, when you reach a junction with a trail to your right. At 1.9 miles, come to a wide opening and trail intersection and turn right on a narrow trail moving gently uphill. At 2.2 miles, turn right at the junction. Continue on, turning left at junctions at 2.3 miles and (nearly) 2.4 miles.

At the intersection at 2.5 miles, stay to the right on the wide trail. On clear days, you will be able to see many of the county's mountains and neighborhoods. Continue straight on the wide trail until you reach your starting point.

GO FARTHER

Carmel Mountain Preserve can be linked to nearby Los Peñasquitos Canyon Preserve, Shaw Valley Open Space, Del Mar Mesa Preserve, and the State Route 56 Bike Path.

12 Del Mar Mesa Preserve

DISTANCE: 4.4 miles roundtrip
ELEVATION GAIN: 370 feet
HIGH POINT: 440 feet
DIFFICULTY: Moderate
FITNESS: Walkers, runners, and cyclists
FAMILY-FRIENDLY: Yes
DOG-FRIENDLY: Yes, leashed
BIKE-FRIENDLY: Yes
AMENITIES: Water and restrooms
CONTACT: City of San Diego
GPS: 32.94324°, –117.17839°

GETTING THERE

Map to: Rancho Toyon Pl., San Diego, CA 92130
Public Transit: None
Parking: Street parking can be found along Rancho Toyon Place and Toyon Mesa Court.

For many years, the Del Mar Mesa Preserve was officially closed to recreation, but finally, in 2015, access was granted to a portion of it. While some of the more sensitive vernal pools and their surrounding habitats are still off-limits, the various open trails allow you to explore some pools. Beyond that, you'll also travel through old-growth coastal chaparral, riparian woodlands, and a dense forest of scrub oak. This area is very popular with mountain bikers, so take extra care to listen for them, especially on singletrack trails.

GET MOVING

Head east on a dirt trail lined with a wooden fence that runs along the south side of Rancho Toyon Place, past some very high-end homes on your left. After 0.8 mile, you will see a kiosk and mountain-bike repair stand at the formal edge of

the preserve. Take the fire road up the slight hill to the next junction. The left fork takes you onto the Bowtie Rim Trail, which reconnects with this fire road. Instead, keep to the right to continue east. If there have been recent rains, you should start to see some of the vernal pools, which harbor not only tadpoles but ephemeral fairy shrimp as well. These tiny shrimp come to life when the pools are filled; otherwise, they remain dormant. If the pools span the entire road, you are advised not to wade through them or into the surrounding chaparral.

At 1.2 miles, you will come to a four-way junction. If you are not interested in continuing down and then up to Deer Creek, take the Bowtie Rim Trail back by turning left here; otherwise, continue straight along the fire road. The trail will remain nice and flat before steeply descending what is known as Cardiac Hill. At the base of the hill, you will cross the seasonal Deer Creek, then begin a short climb up the other side

Whimsical Tunnel 4 Trail in the Del Mar Mesa Preserve

of the canyon to a sign for Deer Canyon. Follow this trail eastward for 0.3 mile to an unsigned junction leading to the right. You now leave the coastal chaparral behind and enter a forest of scrub oak. While most of the oaks only reach about ten to fifteen feet in height, they form a dense, twisted canopy. After crossing Deer Creek again, the trail turns south and begins climbing up a ravine on what is known as Tunnel 4. A warning sign reminds you to be aware of mountain bikers. This portion of the trail is a narrow singletrack, and it can be hard to move out of the way. At 3 miles, leave the oaks and the manzanita behind and return to the mesa near a grove of eucalyptus trees. If you have ever driven across State Route

56 and seen trees off to the south near Camino del Sur, these are those trees.

Feel free to take a well-earned break in the shade before continuing. Follow the service road back toward the west until you reach the four-way junction from earlier. Here you can take the Bowtie Rim Trail (0.5 mile) or the fire road (0.2 mile) back to the preserve's western edge. The Bowtie Rim Trail is singletrack, so you will have to stay vigilant for mountain bikers if you choose this option, but it does offer better scenery along the way. Once you reach the edge of the preserve, follow the community trail back to the start.

GO FARTHER

From the western edge of the preserve, follow the service road southward into Los Peñasquitos Canyon near Carson's Crossing.

13 Los Peñasquitos Canyon Preserve

DISTANCE: 6 miles roundtrip
ELEVATION GAIN: 260 feet
HIGH POINT: 260 feet
DIFFICULTY: Easy to moderate
FITNESS: Walkers, hikers, runners, and cyclists
FAMILY-FRIENDLY: Yes
DOG-FRIENDLY: Yes, leashed
BIKE-FRIENDLY: Yes, but prohibited on singletrack trails
AMENITIES: Restrooms and water
CONTACT: Los Peñasquitos Canyon Preserve
GPS: 32.94031°, -117.13569°
BEFORE YOU GO: Trails open daily, 6 AM–11 PM. After rain, check with park to ensure trails are open and creek crossings have not been damaged.

GETTING THERE

Map to: Peñasquitos Canyon trail head

Public Transit: None

Parking: From Black Mountain Road, turn west onto Canyonside Park Driveway. Go past the first parking lot and continue west past the playground, toward the Los Peñasquitos Ranch House. Just past the last baseball field, you will see a parking area to your right. If you follow this road around the fields, you will find the restrooms and water fountains.

Los Peñasquitos (meaning "little cliffs") Canyon is one of the more popular hikes in San Diego, due mostly to the easily accessible waterfall that sits halfway down the canyon. There are approximately 12 miles of trails in this 3700-acre preserve. Trails flank both sides of the canyon, and bridges make crossing Peñasquitos Creek easy.

GET MOVING

From the southwest corner of Canyonside Community Park, follow the driveway to the west to the historic Los Peñasquitos Ranch House, which is documented as the second-oldest residence in the County of San Diego. A fire in 1912 destroyed the original building, so these are the rebuilt structures. Water fountains and restrooms are available when the grounds are open. If you are hiking when the grounds are closed, proceed to the north end of the parking area and begin your hike along the North Side Trail instead.

At 0.2 mile, find the sign for the ranch house and trail. After exploring the ranch house, return to this junction and follow the trail that begins just past the end of the white fence. At 0.3 mile, reach the North Side Trail. Turn left and head west. There will be a sign indicating 1.9 miles to Carson's Crossing and 2.8 miles to the waterfall. At 0.4 mile from the start, the trail branches at a Y junction. If you are on a bike or with a dog, or if you prefer a wider trail, continue straight, paralleling

Taking a moment to admire the waterfall at Los Peñasquitos Canyon

the backyards of houses along the route. If you want a more secluded hike, take the trail to the left (southwest) to reach the singletrack closer to the creek, which passes oak and sycamore trees. Watch for poison oak, which grows in abundance near the water and at times sprawls onto the trail. Whichever route you choose, work your way westward toward the waterfall.

For this hike, we will continue straight along the wider trail. During spring, you will find a variety of wildflowers blooming across the grassland sections of the canyon. At 1.25 miles, reach another Y junction. Continue straight, since the right branch accesses Park Village Road. Occasionally, you will pass trails leading south; these are connectors to the path

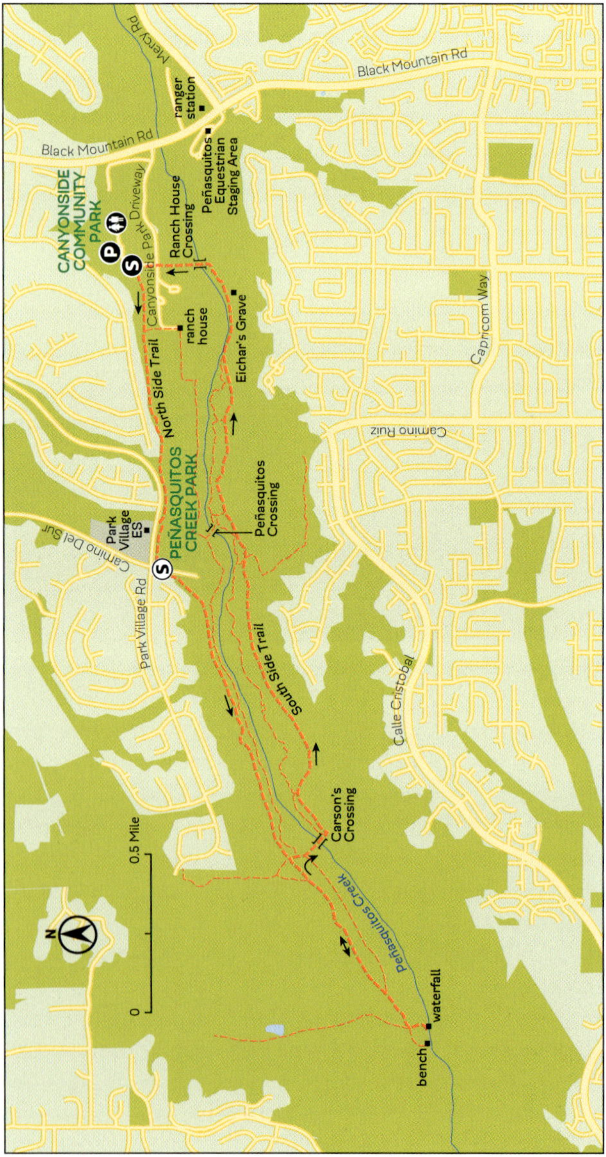

Black Mountain Rd
Mercy Rd
ranger station
Peñasquitos Equestrian Staging Area
Ranch House Crossing
CANYONSIDE COMMUNITY PARK
Canyonside Park Driveway
ranch house
Eichar's Grave
North Side Trail
Capricorn Way
Camino Ruiz
PEÑASQUITOS CREEK PARK
Peñasquitos Crossing
Park Village ES
Camino Del Sur
Park Village Rd
South Side Trail
Calle Cristobal
Carson's Crossing
Peñasquitos Creek
waterfall
bench
0
0.5 Mile
N

along the creek. Soon, cross a small bridge and reach the eastern edge of Peñasquitos Creek Park. Another short spur trail leads to the right and up to Park Village Road. Ignore it and instead follow the path south to a sign for the Peñasquitos Park Creek Crossing, one of several designated crossings scattered along the canyon. You will not use this crossing; instead, continue following the trail west.

At 2.2 miles, reach the junction for Carson's Crossing. The waterfall is just another 0.75 mile to the west. As you approach a small rocky mound, you will see the sign to the waterfall. Follow the trail south for about 400 feet to a nice view of the falls. Feel free to scramble down to the water or simply sit and enjoy the view. The water is mostly urban runoff, so playing in it is not recommended. While you can carefully cross the creek if the flow is low enough, we suggest using one of the designated crossings you passed earlier. There is a nice bench a bit farther to the west. To reach it, return to the North Side Trail, continue briefly west, then take the first trail to the left. This spot offers a more peaceful view of the falls.

Return to Carson's Crossing and use the long wooden bridge and boardwalk to cross the creek safely. If you are hiking after a rainstorm, check with the park rangers about the status of each creek crossing you might choose. Bridges have washed away in the past. Once across the creek, turn left and head east along the South Side Trail. Just like on the north side, you can choose from a wide trail or singletrack. The main trail tends to be rocky, as it is closer to the actual creek and more prone to flooding. As you go, look for various animals that live in the canyon: mule deer, raccoons, or maybe even a bobcat.

At 5.7 miles, look for a sign pointing to Eichar's Grave, a memorial tombstone placed in honor of the 1800s-era cook at the ranch house. There are several benches here to take a well-earned break in the shade. Continue along the trail to the Ranch House Crossing. Take it north across the creek and find yourself at the trailhead where you began. If you skipped visiting the ranch house at the start of the hike, take the connector trail to your left just after the crossing. Otherwise, continue straight back to the parking area.

GO FARTHER

The trails in Peñasquitos Canyon continue westward to Interstate 5 for another 3 miles. You can also connect north to the Del Mar Mesa Preserve from trails near the Carson's Crossing junction.

14 Lopez Canyon

DISTANCE:	4 miles roundtrip
ELEVATION GAIN:	160 feet
HIGH POINT:	210 feet
DIFFICULTY:	Easy
FITNESS:	Hikers, runners, and cyclists
FAMILY-FRIENDLY:	Yes
DOG-FRIENDLY:	Yes, leashed
BIKE-FRIENDLY:	Yes
AMENITIES:	Restrooms and picnic tables
CONTACT:	City of San Diego
GPS:	32.90648°, -117.20611°
BEFORE YOU GO:	After rain, check with park to make sure trails are open and creek crossings have not been damaged. Trails open daily, 6 AM–11 PM.

GETTING THERE

Map to: 4300 Sorrento Valley Blvd., San Diego, CA 92121
Public Transit: None
Parking: A large dirt parking lot is located on the south side of Sorrento Valley Boulevard.

Lopez Canyon is a small side canyon next to the western end of Los Peñasquitos Canyon. This trail follows the seasonal

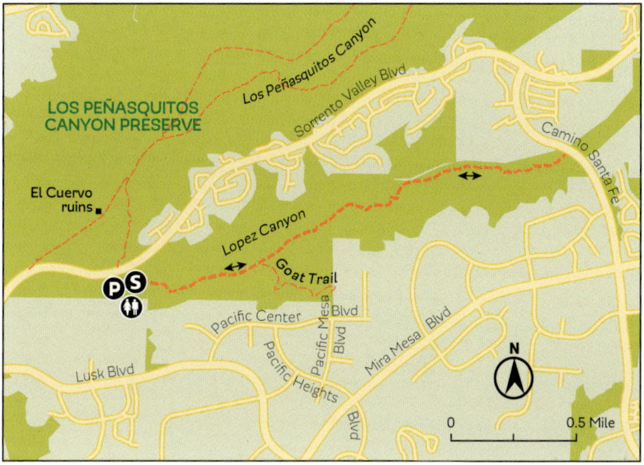

Lopez Creek, allowing you to enjoy some lovely riparian habitat while escaping the usually busier Los Peñasquitos Canyon trails.

GET MOVING

Start on the trailhead at the eastern end of the parking lot. After 0.1 mile, reach a T intersection and an information kiosk. The left fork passes under Sorrento Valley Boulevard and into Peñasquitos Canyon (an alternate route to the waterfall). Instead, take the right fork through some grassy open space before the trail curves to the right and makes one of its first creek crossings. Unlike Peñasquitos Canyon, there are no bridges across this creek, so if the water is flowing, you might have difficulty hiking this trail. Lopez Creek is seasonal, so most likely it will be dry.

Pass willow trees, mule-fat shrubs, and other plants (including poison oak) as you make your way eastward. This wide trail is actually an old service road. The steep canyon wall will be directly on your right, and the creek to your left. After about 0.6 mile, the trail splits again. The right fork follows

Dry summertime conditions in Lopez Canyon

an old dirt road up and out of the canyon to the nearby office buildings. Instead, continue straight, following the creek.

The trail will cross the creek bed from time to time as it continues working eastward. Occasional sycamore trees offer some welcome shade. At about 1.1 miles from the trailhead, another side trail, the Goat Trail, will lead up and out of the canyon and into Sorrento Mesa. Again, stay in the main canyon and continue eastward. At around 1.5 miles, the trail will vanish into the smooth, rocky streambed of Lopez Creek. Off in the distance, you will be able to see Camino Santa Fe crossing over the canyon.

Depending on your desire to hike on this terrain for a short while, you might want to turn around at this point. If you care to continue on, walk through the streambed for 0.1 mile, keeping an eye out for a singletrack trail leading off to the left. You'll spot it right after the stream makes a noticeable bend, and before it makes another bend. You can follow this trail almost to the base of the bridge without risking turning an ankle in the streambed. When you are ready to return, simply retrace your route. One word of caution—when I hiked this trail, I had several encounters with ticks on both myself and my dog, so take care to check everyone for unwelcome hitchhikers.

GO FARTHER

Just 0.3 mile down Sorrento Valley Boulevard sits the El Cuervo (The Crow) adobe ruins. From the parking lot, head west along the road until you see a trail entrance on the north side. Cross the road carefully, then walk another 0.1 mile to the ruins. A covering protects them from some of the elements. This adobe was constructed around 1857 and is one of the oldest existing adobes in Southern California.

15 Lake Miramar

DISTANCE: 4.9 miles roundtrip
ELEVATION GAIN: 90 feet
HIGH POINT: 750 feet
DIFFICULTY: Easy
FITNESS: Walkers, runners, and cyclists
FAMILY-FRIENDLY: Yes
DOG-FRIENDLY: Yes, leashed and at least 50 feet away from water
BIKE-FRIENDLY: Yes
AMENITIES: Restrooms, water, and picnic tables
CONTACT: City of San Diego
GPS: 32.91353°, –117.09966°
BEFORE YOU GO: Open daily from sunrise to sunset. Lake Miramar is closed the first Tuesday of each month.

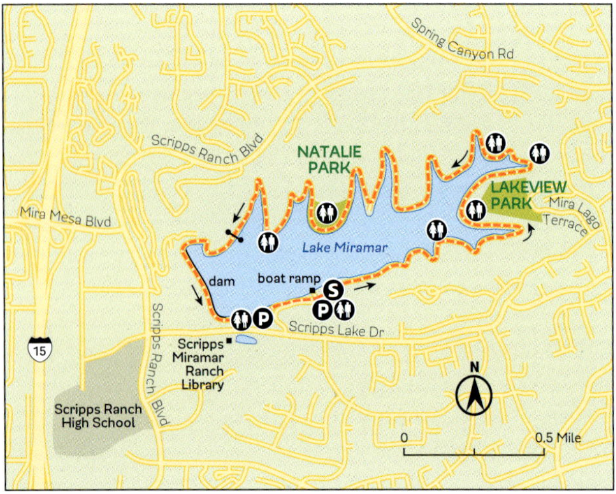

GETTING THERE

Map to: 10305 Scripps Lake Dr., San Diego, CA 92131

Public Transit: None

Parking: After making a left turn from Scripps Lake Drive to the access road for Lake Miramar, you will see the first parking area to your left. This parking lot has no amenities. Follow the access road to the main parking lot, where you will find more parking, the boat ramp, and the Lake Miramar Concession.

The Lake Miramar reservoir was built in 1960 and serves as the source of water for northern San Diego. As such, human contact with the water is prohibited, but boating and fishing are okay. The lake is located in Scripps Ranch, which was owned by newspaper publisher E. W. Scripps and his sister, Ellen Browning Scripps. When the property was purchased in 1890, there were no buildings to obstruct the view of Mount Soledad and the Pacific Ocean, so it was named Miramar, meaning "sea view."

The loop at Lake Miramar is popular for walking, jogging, and cycling.

GET MOVING

Since this hike is usually done as a loop, the direction around the lake is up to you. This description follows a counterclockwise route. The trail is very popular with runners and bicyclists, so keep an ear out for other trail users approaching from behind.

After the boat ramp and concession stand, the trail splits between a dirt path closer to the water and a paved road. Both follow the contours of the lakeshore, with trail markers every quarter mile and chemical toilets roughly every half mile. As you make your way eastward, watch for birds such as mallards, ruddy ducks, cormorants, and pelicans, who also might be enjoying the lake. After about 1.2 miles from the boat ramp, you'll see Lakeview Park sitting above you on a small hill. There are side trails to make the 50-foot climb up to it. From either up at the park or from the trail, this is a great spot to look across the length of the reservoir.

Continue along the path of your choice, now turning mostly back to the west. During your journey along the fingers and inlets of the lake, you should spy a nice variety of plants, including black sage, manzanita, chamise, and coastal sagebrush. At the 3.5-mile mark (assuming you are taking the counterclockwise route), you will reach Natalie Park, a nice spot to take a break at one of the picnic tables or under one of the trees; restrooms are located just to the west. This park also offers barbecue grills, and a small fishing pier sits just to the south. It is possible to drive to this park, so don't be alarmed if a car passes by you. Note: vehicles are only allowed on the road Saturday through Tuesday.

Continuing along the trail, pass another small fishing pier, where you will probably see people fishing for bass, bluegill, or sunfish. As you approach the dam, fencing lines the trail on both sides to protect access to it and the lake. Crossing the dam, you will have a good view of the communities of Miramar and Mira Mesa. If it is a clear day, you should also be able to make out the Pacific Ocean. Once across the dam, continue on the trail and return to where you started.

GO FARTHER

If you want to explore the area a bit more, try Evans Pond near the Scripps Miramar Ranch Library, just to the south of where you turned onto the access road. This small pond is home to frogs and turtles, so as you follow the dirt path around its shoreline, keep an eye out. If the library is open, you can purchase food to feed the ducks and other birds (bread is not recommended).

OPPOSITE: *Junipero Serra Museum is the site of the first permanent European settlement in the present-day State of California (Trail 20).*

CENTRAL

16 Rose Canyon

DISTANCE: 5.3 miles roundtrip
ELEVATION GAIN: 140 feet
HIGH POINT: 240 feet
DIFFICULTY: Moderate
FITNESS: Hikers, runners, and cyclists
FAMILY-FRIENDLY: Yes
DOG-FRIENDLY: Yes, leashed
BIKE-FRIENDLY: Yes
AMENITIES: None
CONTACT: City of San Diego
GPS: 32.86045°, -117.20882°
BEFORE YOU GO: This trail is popular with mountain bikers; take caution in the few sections of singletrack trail.

GETTING THERE

Map to: 7042 Genesee Ave., San Diego, CA 92122

Public Transit: Take MTS Bus Route 41 or 105 to Genesee Avenue and Centurion Square. Walk south on Genesee to the sign at the entrance of Rose Canyon on the west side of the street.

Parking: From Genesee Avenue, turn onto Decoro Street and find free street parking. Walk 0.4 mile south on Genesee Avenue to the trailhead. There are alternate trailheads on Regents Road and Bloch Street.

Rose Canyon is located in the University City area of San Diego. Its interesting past began thousands of years ago when the Kumeyaay inhabited a seasonal village here. In 1853, the canyon's namesake, Louis Rose, purchased about 650 acres of land and built a ranch and a tannery, planted a vineyard, and mined coal deposits and clay. In 1882, the California Southern Railroad completed a track through the canyon, and it was used commercially until the 1960s, when the last structures were removed. Today, Rose Canyon has been set aside for nature study, bird-watching, and recreation, including hiking, running, mountain biking, and walking pets on the relatively flat, smooth, long trail.

GET MOVING

Begin your trip at the signed entrance to Rose Canyon Open Space Park. Enter to the side of the metal gate and follow the wide trail as it descends into the shaded canyon. After a short distance, come to a nature trail to the left; continue straight on the main trail. Take care, as there is a significant amount of poison oak here, but it is easy to avoid due to the large width of the trail. After about a quarter mile, leave the shaded tree canopy and follow the trail as it becomes more exposed.

As you walk, take note of the plants around you. Rose Canyon is diverse, with four different habitats throughout the park: chaparral and coastal sage scrub cover hills and fields,

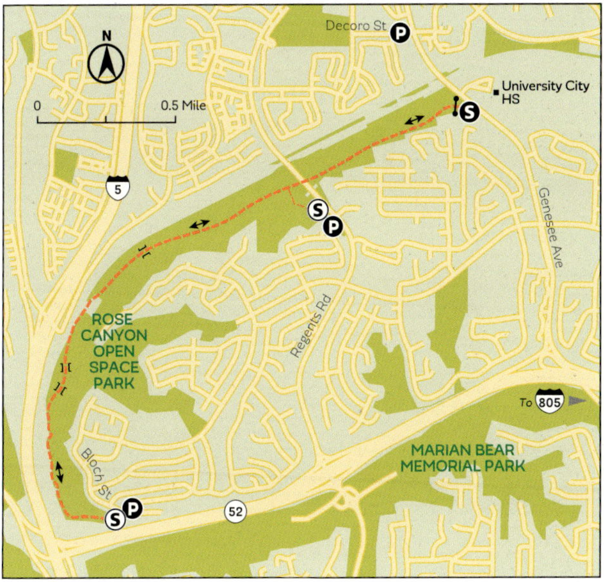

Hiking through the shade of the tree canopy at Rose Canyon

oak woodlands are visible on the north-facing hillsides, and a rare riparian habitat runs the length of the park. Rose Creek is visible in small glimpses as it naturally meanders around the canyon floor. This is part of the Rose Canyon Watershed, starting from runoff on the western slopes of Scripps Ranch, traveling through Marine Corps Air Station Miramar before joining with San Clemente and Stevenson Canyons and their tributaries, and emptying into Mission Bay.

At this point on the trail, you may see or hear trains traveling on tracks to the right. Focus on the sounds from the wildlife—the mammals, birds, insects, and amphibians that call this place home. After 0.8 mile, continue straight past the trail junction to Regents Road to the left. At around 1.2 miles, cross over a bridge—one of several in place to help keep your feet dry when the creek is full. Here, the trail becomes rockier. This is a good turnaround point for a shorter hike.

Otherwise, follow the trail as it veers left along railroad tracks, Interstate 5, and the Rose Canyon Fault. You will notice an informal trail to the right that is used to cross the train tracks and join the Rose Canyon Bikeway. Continue along the main trail and, at 1.9 miles, follow the trail as it narrows to singletrack and passes through a shaded area. Cross over two bridges before emerging from the tree cover.

Begin climbing an exposed hill toward some powerlines. Here, you will be able to see I-5 to the right and State Route 52 in front of you. Crest the hill and descend down the opposite side. At 2.5 miles, come to a trail junction to Marian Bear Memorial Park to the right. Continue straight another 0.2 mile to the end of the trail at Bloch Street. Turn around and retrace your steps back to the starting point.

GO FARTHER

Rose Canyon has connections to the trail network at Marian Bear Memorial Park and to the Rose Creek Bikeway.

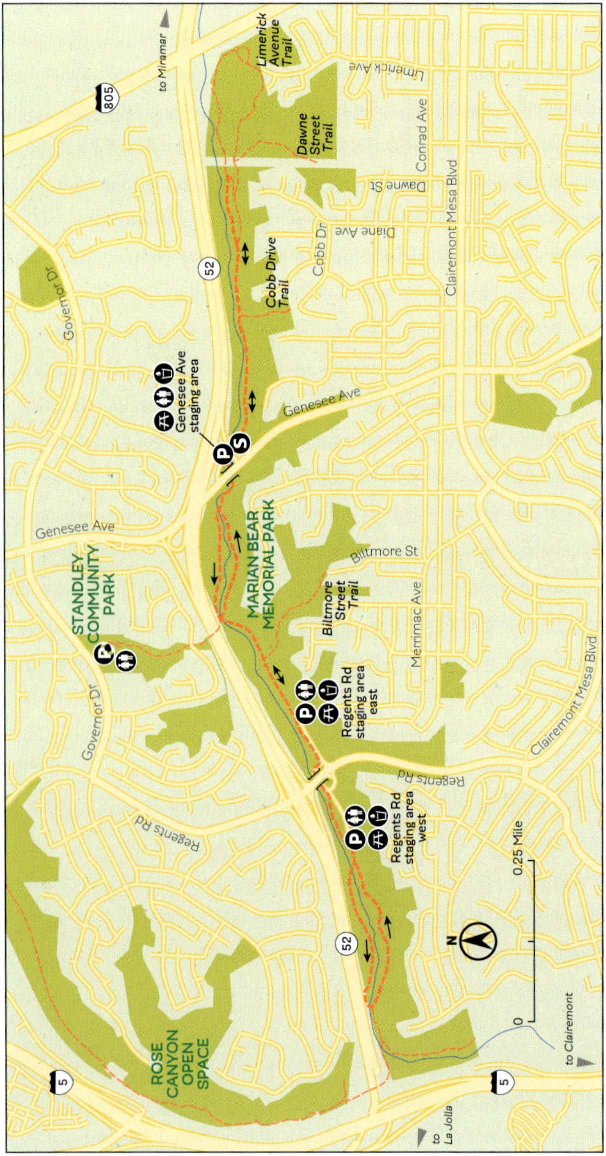

to Miramar
805
Limerick Avenue Trail
Limerick Ave
Dawne Street Trail
Conrad Ave
Dawne St
Clairemont Mesa Blvd
Diane Ave
Cobb Dr
Cobb Drive Trail
52
Governor Dr
Genesee Ave staging area
Genesee Ave
MARIAN BEAR MEMORIAL PARK
STANDLEY COMMUNITY PARK
Biltmore St
Biltmore Street Trail
Merrimac Ave
Regents Rd staging area east
Regents Rd
Regents Rd staging area west
Clairemont Mesa Blvd
0
0.25 Mile
N
ROSE CANYON OPEN SPACE
5
to La Jolla
to Clairemont

17 Marian Bear Memorial Park

DISTANCE:	6.1 miles roundtrip
ELEVATION GAIN:	130 feet
HIGH POINT:	260 feet
DIFFICULTY:	Easy to moderate
FITNESS:	Hikers, runners, and cyclists
FAMILY-FRIENDLY:	Yes
DOG-FRIENDLY:	Yes, leashed
BIKE-FRIENDLY:	Yes
AMENITIES:	Restrooms, picnic tables, and water
CONTACT:	City of San Diego
GPS:	32.84559°, -117.19974°
BEFORE YOU GO:	Trail requires seasonal creek crossings, which can be impassable after significant rainfall. Popular with mountain bikers; take caution on the sections of singletrack trail.

GETTING THERE

Map to: 5491 Genesee Ave., San Diego, CA 92117

Public Transit: Take MTS Bus Route 41 to the entrance of Marian Bear Memorial Park on Genesee Avenue.

Parking: From Genesee Avenue, turn into the large lot and find free parking. There are two additional staging areas with large parking lots on both sides of Regents Road. Parking lot gates are open 5:30 AM–8:00 PM.

San Clemente Canyon lies just south of State Route 52, between Interstates 5 and 805. SR 52 was originally planned to run through the canyon, but thanks to the efforts of community leader and environmentalist Marian Bear, the canyon was preserved and SR 52 was realigned to its current location. Most of San Clemente Canyon is now within Marian Bear Memorial Park. There are entry points off Genesee Avenue and Regents Road, creating three separate segments:

Wildflower-lined San Clemente Canyon in spring

between Genesee Avenue and I-805, between Genesee Avenue and Regents Road, and between Regents Road and I-5; all staging areas have parking lots, picnic areas, water, and restrooms.

This route from the Genesee trailhead consists of mostly flat trails along the canyon, following the tree canopy and creek. This is one of San Diego's best examples of riparian woodland habitat, with dense year-round vegetation, water resources, and wildlife.

GET MOVING

From the Genesee Avenue staging area, head east past the information kiosk, restroom, and water fountain, following signs for Limerick Avenue. Walk under the overpass and descend to a creek crossing, which varies based on time of year and rainfall, ranging from hopping over cobblestones in the summer to shallow-water wading in the winter. Though there is always water, it is usually easiest to cross at the far right. Continue on the wide trail as it curves left. Along the canyon, oak, sycamore, and willow trees create shade and block the sight and sound of cars on the highway. Native plants and other species—including poison oak—line the trail. Pass the trail junction to Cobb Drive at 0.5 mile, continuing straight. At around one mile, reach the junction to Conrad and Regina Avenues. This is a good place to turn around and head back to the staging area, as the trail becomes narrow and overgrown past this point.

Retrace the route back to the Genesee Avenue staging area. Just before the parking lot, veer left, taking the trail downhill to the underpass. Walk along the right side, taking care because the path is uneven and requires navigating rocks. Turn right on the trail to continue toward Regents Road. After a short distance, cross the creek and follow the trail to the right. Reach a fork, with both routes indicating Regents Road. Take the trail to the right. The sections between Genesee Avenue and Regents Road, and Regents Road and I-5, have trails paralleling each other, providing the opportunity to create loops. Follow this route or choose your own trail, moving in the same general direction.

After a short distance, cross the creek again. At the junction to Standley Community Park, stay left and continue toward Regents Road. At a large water crossing, follow the faint trail to the right for the path of least resistance through the water. After crossing, veer left at the fork before turning right onto the wide trail. Next, turn left on the signed trail to Regents Road. Here, notice the steep canyon wall to the left. The hillsides are covered in coastal sage scrub and chaparral.

After about 0.9 mile from Genesee Avenue, reach the Regents Road staging area east, with restrooms, an information kiosk, drinking fountains, benches, and a large parking lot. Take the trail to the right of the lot, following signs for Rose Canyon. Continue to a paved path with blocked vehicle access. Turn right and follow the road under the overpass, then take the trail to the right. Follow it as it parallels the parking lot, and pass restrooms on the right at around 3.5 miles. Take the trail to the right at the junction labeled Park Boundary and Rose Canyon and continue west. This section is narrow, with more brush, but it is a good place to see wildlife, including raccoons, coyotes, foxes, skunks, rabbits, amphibians, reptiles, and birds. Just past 4 miles, cross the creek again and follow the trail to the left. Take another left to head east back to the starting point. Though there are additional trails to the right, heading toward I-5 and Rose Canyon, this is a good turnaround spot.

Follow the trail as it gently moves through rolling hills and tree tunnels. Close the loop and pass the restrooms at the Regents Road staging area west. Walk under the overpass and turn left, retracing your steps back to the Regents Road staging area east. About 0.4 mile past the staging area, take the trail to the right over a newly built bridge and wooden platform for 0.2 mile to another junction. Take the trail to the left, eventually rejoining the main trail east toward Genesee Avenue. Cross the creek and continue, then turn left and maneuver through the underpass again. Exit and use the trail to the left to climb back up to the starting point.

GO FARTHER

Add on additional miles by exploring any of the several finger canyons leading up to the mesa tops. At the park's western terminus, you can also take a multi-canyon adventure by continuing on the trail in Rose Canyon.

18 Tecolote Canyon

DISTANCE: 6.4 miles roundtrip
ELEVATION GAIN: 390 feet
HIGH POINT: 210 feet
DIFFICULTY: Moderate
FITNESS: Hikers, runners, and cyclists
FAMILY-FRIENDLY: Yes
DOG-FRIENDLY: Yes, leashed
BIKE-FRIENDLY: Yes
AMENITIES: Restrooms and water
CONTACT: City of San Diego
GPS: 32.77575°, –117.19751°

GETTING THERE

Map to: Tecolote Canyon trailhead
Public Transit: The MTS Blue Line Trolley stops at the Tecolote Road Station. Walk north to Tecolote Road, then east for about 0.6 mile until you reach the Tecolote Nature Center. MTS Bus Route 105 stops at Morena Boulevard and Viola Street. Continue north along Morena, turn right onto Tecolote Road, and follow it east for about 0.5 mile to the Tecolote Nature Center.
Parking: There is plenty of free parking along Tecolote Road.

Tucked away just east of Mission Bay is Tecolote Canyon (*tecolote* is Spanish for "owl"). It is actually a collection of many canyons, now separated by several major roads. This hike explores what is known as Tecolote Canyon South. The Kumeyaay people used this area to gather food and for shelter before the arrival of the first European settler, Judge Hyde, who began farming in 1872 after building his home here. In fact, cattle were still grazing in the canyon until 1953.

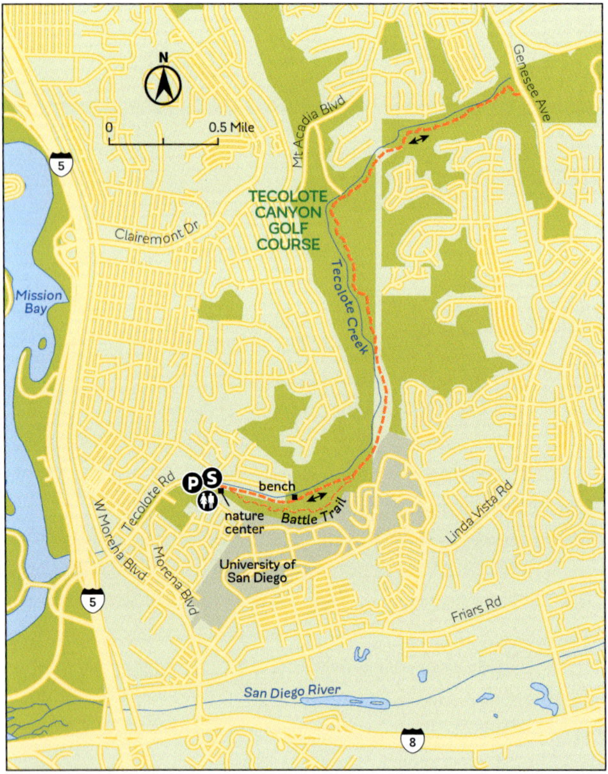

GET MOVING

From the Tecolote Nature Center, the trail starts along a wide gravel path before transitioning to dirt. Coastal scrub lines the side trail as you make your way eastward. At 0.1 mile, the singletrack Battle Trail branches off to the right. This trail was named in honor of Eloise Battle, who helped establish Tecolote Canyon as a natural preserve, and it reconnects with the main trail in 0.6 mile. Above, on the mesa to your right, lies the University of San Diego and the distinctive blue dome of its church. Soon, pass a large sycamore tree with a nice bench.

Tecolote Canyon on an overcast morning

Since there is not a lot of shade on this trail, this is a great place to stop and apply your sunscreen if you forgot earlier.

The trail gently turns northward, and if Tecolote Creek is flowing, you should be able to catch glimpses of it from time to time. At around 0.9 mile, an access road connects from the right to the powerlines passing through this portion of the canyon. At 1.3 miles, the trail forks again. Stay to the left along the singletrack, which follows the boundary of the Tecolote Canyon Golf Course. This portion of the trail involves a modest amount of steep ups and downs.

At 2 miles, the trail once again turns eastward and leaves the uninspiring views of the golf course behind. Here it returns to singletrack as it passes through a small oak forest. Keep an eye out to your left, as a rope swing is usually hanging from one of the oaks over the creek. Feel free to take a break for some fun!

As the trail continues to make its way eastward, you'll make a few creek crossings. Depending on the time of year, it may be completely dry or flowing. Be mindful of poison oak, as it grows near the creek's edge. The trail alternates between the shade of oak trees and coastal scrub. Soon, the din of traffic starts to replace the quiet of the canyon, meaning you have almost reached Genesee Avenue. Once at the trail's end, simply turn around and retrace your route back to the nature center.

19 San Diego River Trail

DISTANCE: 1.9 miles roundtrip
ELEVATION GAIN: Minimal
HIGH POINT: 70 feet
DIFFICULTY: Easy
FITNESS: Walkers, runners, and cyclists
FAMILY-FRIENDLY: Yes
DOG-FRIENDLY: Yes, leashed
BIKE-FRIENDLY: Yes
AMENITIES: Restrooms, picnic tables, playground, and water
CONTACT: San Diego State University (SDSU) Mission Valley
GPS: 32.77862°, -117.12634°
BEFORE YOU GO: Certain parking areas are closed to the public when there is a stadium event. Parking in the stadium lots is prohibited. All street parking is either metered or time limited.

GETTING THERE

Map to: SDSU Mission Valley River Park, San Diego, CA 92108

Public Transit: Take the MTS Green Line Trolley to the Fenton Parkway Station. Exit the station on Fenton Parkway and turn right to enter the San Diego River Trail.

Parking: From Friars Road, turn onto River Park Road and follow the road south. Two-hour parking is available on River Park Road, south of the trolley and parallel to the park. The rest of the parking is metered through the PayByPhone mobile app.

The Mission Valley area is named for California's first Spanish mission, San Diego de Alcalá, established in 1769 and still operating as a Catholic parish in a reconstructed building. Mission Valley is split by the San Diego River, which travels approximately 52 miles from the mountains of Julian to the Pacific Ocean.

Hikers enjoy shade from the elevated trolley line.

In 2020, San Diego State University purchased the land where the former stadium sat from the city. The university has redeveloped the site and adjacent San Diego River Park into SDSU Mission Valley, with more than 80 acres of community parks and open space, including 34-acre River Park that opened in December 2023. This 1.9-mile loop, which includes part of the Ben and Nikki Clay San Diego River Trail, winds through River Park and encircles the SDSU Mission Valley site. When complete, this new, vital portion of the San Diego River Trail will connect the mountains to the ocean.

GET MOVING

This route generally follows the park's perimeter. Begin on the sidewalk at the south side of River Park Road and Fenton

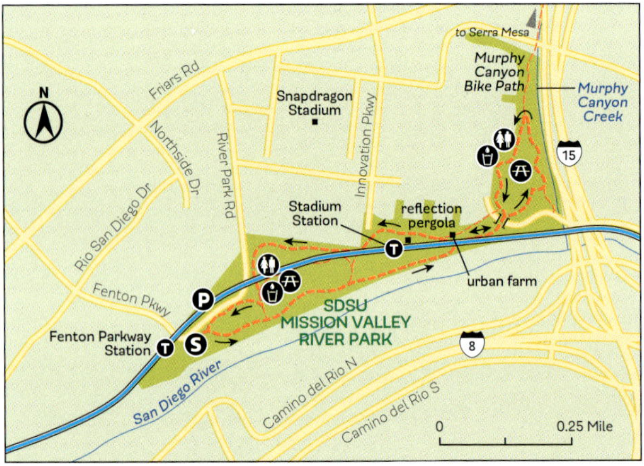

Parkway. Follow the paved path to the right onto the Ben and Nikki Clay San Diego River Trail. You can stay on the concrete walkway or take the dirt path parallel to the pavement. There are also several small dirt trails winding through a mixture of preexisting and landscaped drought-resistant native plant gardens. Watch for plants like the California poppy, California sycamore, California wildrose, coastal agave, coast live oak, Mojave yucca, San Diego sunflower, and white sage. Eleven interpretive panels are scattered throughout the park, with information ranging from Kumeyaay history to animals of the San Diego River.

Stay right, following the southern perimeter of the park. To the right, the San Diego River is fenced off to protect the sensitive habitat and therefore is largely invisible. The San Diego River valley is a natural floodplain; flooding here has created challenges for farmers in the past and is a current obstacle for business, housing, and hotel development. The new River Park is designed to act as a green sponge through its grading plan and storm-drain system, which collect and treat runoff, directing drainage to retention basins before it travels to the river.

To the left, elevated trolley tracks rise above a playground with restrooms, basketball courts, a fitness area, picnic tables, benches, and grass fields. At 0.3 mile, take the dirt trail on the right. Walk east toward San Diego's high point, Cowles Mountain, visible in the distance. Cross underneath the elevated trolley tracks and bear right to continue walking under the tracks. Follow the path through a tunnel and move right after exiting. At 0.8 mile, cross a footbridge and turn left to follow the path north.

Here, walk parallel to Interstate 15 and one of the San Diego River's tributaries, Murphy Canyon Creek. At around 0.9 mile, reach the Murphy Canyon Bike Path. On the left, look for a faint dirt trail. Take a sharp left here and follow the trail back to the park. At 1 mile, return to the pavement and follow the path right. Pass restrooms and curve left, following the large grassy area until you reach the tunnel again.

Turn right to go through the tunnel. After exiting, walk alongside the trolley tracks, passing the MAKE Projects' urban farm on the right. Loop around the trolley plaza, admiring its central focal point, the Mike and Christine Pack Reflection Pergola, which draws inspiration from the river and *ewaa* (dome-shaped shelters) used by the Kumeyaay. At Innovation Parkway, turn left. Walk toward the trolley tracks and turn right to join the path on the north side of the tracks. Continue on, checking out the various courts and fitness equipment beneath the tracks. At River Park Road, curve left past another restroom. Cross underneath the trolley tracks and continue straight. At 1.8 miles, turn right and follow the path back to the starting point.

GO FARTHER

This park was designed for laps, with mileage markers located every quarter mile along the loop. Other options for a longer outing are continuing on the Murphy Canyon Bike Path or using city streets to connect to other segments of the regional San Diego River Trail system within Mission Valley.

An unusual staircase along the trail in Presidio Park

20 Presidio Park Loop

DISTANCE: 1.7 miles roundtrip
ELEVATION GAIN: 140 feet
HIGH POINT: 170 feet
DIFFICULTY: Easy
FITNESS: Hikers and runners
FAMILY-FRIENDLY: Yes
DOG-FRIENDLY: Yes, leashed
BIKE-FRIENDLY: No
AMENITIES: Restrooms, picnic tables, and water
CONTACT: City of San Diego
GPS: 32.75661°, -117.19497°
BEFORE YOU GO: Public park open dawn–11 PM; museum open 10 AM–4 PM. There are often unhoused individuals along this trail. While we did not feel unsafe at any point, if it makes you uncomfortable, plan to do this one with a buddy.

GETTING THERE

Map to: Old Town San Diego State Park
Public Transit: From the Old Town Transit Center, walk northeast along Taylor Street, then turn right onto Juan Street. After two blocks, turn left onto Mason Street, then follow it to Jackson Street and the start of the hike.
Parking: There is some on-street parking along Juan Street. You will typically have to use one of the many parking lots for Old Town San Diego State Park.

George W. Marston, a local civic leader, purchased Presidio Hill in 1907. His intention was to preserve this area due to its historical significance, as this was where Spanish explorers in 1769 established what eventually became the San Diego Presidio and Mission San Diego de Alcalá. The Presidio would serve as the capital of Baja California during the area's rule by Mexico, while the mission was moved farther inland to its

current location. Although none of these original structures remain, the park was designated a National Historic Landmark in 1960. The building you see standing prominently on the hill is the Junípero Serra Museum, built in 1928.

GET MOVING

Starting at the intersection of Mason and Jackson Streets, make a short climb up to the loop trail. Turn left to continue making your way toward the Junípero Serra Museum. The trail will fade away, but stroll across the grassy field toward the parking lot near the museum. Two points of interest are located here: the Junípero Serra Cross and the Witches Tower. The cross was built in 1913 with tile fragments from the original Presidio of 1769. The tower, located next to the parking lot, has a pentagram set into its top floor, hence its name. After exploring this part of the park, cross Presidio Drive to pick up the route again. Ignore the brick pathway leading to the museum. Instead, look for the concrete pathway that takes you around it.

After you wrap around the building, Presidio Park will be directly ahead of you. When you reach a wooden gazebo, make a hairpin turn to follow the trail down the ravine toward the north to a small parking lot and restroom. Taylor Street will be directly in front of you. Make another U-turn to climb back up the ravine on the other side. A few bridges cross the drainage channel, so pick your favorite one. As you make your way up the ravine, you will once again make a U-turn at a junction to reach another parking lot.

Once there, head over to a small viewing area looking over Mission Valley to the north. Cross through the parking lot to the south side and notice an open area. The trail will pick up toward the southeast of this open area. Spot a bench up the hill to the east—feel free to walk up and soak in the view.

Once you have again located the trail, head directly south for a short distance before reaching a junction. Continue straight, and after a quick climb, cross the grassy area to Cosoy (Kosa'aay) Way, named after the Kumeyaay village that existed here before the Spanish arrived. Follow this road south for 0.1 mile, past the bronze statue of a Mexican vaquero on horseback, to Marston Gate at the corner of Cosoy Way and Presidio Drive.

The trail continues on the west side of Presidio Drive, but before you head down the hill, you may want to make the short walk to view the Mormon Battalion monument, erected at the site of Fort Stockton. This spot also offers some great views of Mission Bay and Ocean Beach. Once you are done with the views and some history lessons, return to the trail and make your way down the hill to where you began this loop.

GO FARTHER

With Old Town San Diego directly next to the park, there are plenty of opportunities for continued exploration. Heritage Park, a collection of preserved historic Victorian buildings, is a short walk away.

21 Mission Hills Loop

DISTANCE: 3 miles roundtrip
ELEVATION GAIN: 270 feet
HIGH POINT: 300 feet
DIFFICULTY: Easy to moderate
FITNESS: Walkers, hikers, and runners
FAMILY-FRIENDLY: Yes
DOG-FRIENDLY: Yes, leashed
BIKE-FRIENDLY: No
AMENITIES: Restrooms, playground, picnic tables, and water
CONTACT: City of San Diego
GPS: 32.74895°, –117.17834°
BEFORE YOU GO: Portions of the trail in Mission Hills Canyon are overgrown with brush, eroded, narrow, and steep. Trekking poles and long pants are recommended.

GETTING THERE

Map to: 1521 Washington Place, San Diego, CA 92103
Public Transit: Take MTS Bus Route 83 to West Lewis Street and Palmetto Way. Head east on West Lewis. Turn right on Randolph Street and follow it until it meets Washington Place.
Parking: There is a small parking lot at the west end of Pioneer Park. Find free parking here or on the street.

Mission Hills is a historic neighborhood of San Diego, perched on hills overlooking Old Town, downtown San Diego, and San Diego Bay. The neighborhood's manicured streets are primarily residential, with shops and restaurants interspersed in several clusters. Many of its homes date back to the early twentieth century and are preserved as some of the most beautiful in San Diego. The community is also home to several natural canyons and to Mission Hills Park, known by locals as Pioneer Park. This 3-mile loop combines city streets, canyon trails, and park pathways to explore the hidden gems and spooky spots in this unique neighborhood.

Channel your inner Edward Scissorhands *at Harper's Topiary Garden.*

GET MOVING

From the parking lot at Pioneer Park, follow the paved path to the right as it curves counterclockwise around the park, which is a community hub for Mission Hills; it is typically bustling with residents and dogs recreating on its 6 acres of green grass and playground. After about 0.1 mile, look to the right and notice nearly 150 tombstones in the park's southeast corner. Pioneer Park was once the site of the Calvary Cemetery, a Catholic burial ground where the remains of four thousand early San Diego settlers were buried between 1876 and 1960. Though the city removed most of the headstones and converted the land into a park in 1970, most of the bodies remain interred under the manicured grass. Claimed by some to be haunted, this is probably one of the best places for a Halloween hike.

Tombstones are tucked into the corner of Pioneer Park, San Diego's graveyard-turned-park.

Continue past Grant K-8, a playground, and a restroom before exiting the park at the intersection of Washington Place and Randolph Street. Use the crosswalk to turn left on Washington Place. Pass the tennis courts, then take a faint trail to the right, leading you to a sign indicating the start of the Mission Hills Canyon Trail. Also known as Robyn's Egg Trail or Monastery Trail, this path descends for about a half mile through the narrow Mission Hills Canyon before ending at Titus Street.

Take caution here, as this rustic hiking trail requires navigating a rocky creek bed, downed trees, brush overgrowth, and some sections of narrow, eroded, and steep path. The trail winds through grass, trees, and prickly pear cactus. The canyon is particularly green and lovely during the spring, bursting with wildflowers. At the bottom of the trail near Titus Street, you might notice blue planters on the hillside to the left, where San Diego Canyonlands is repairing the damaged streambed

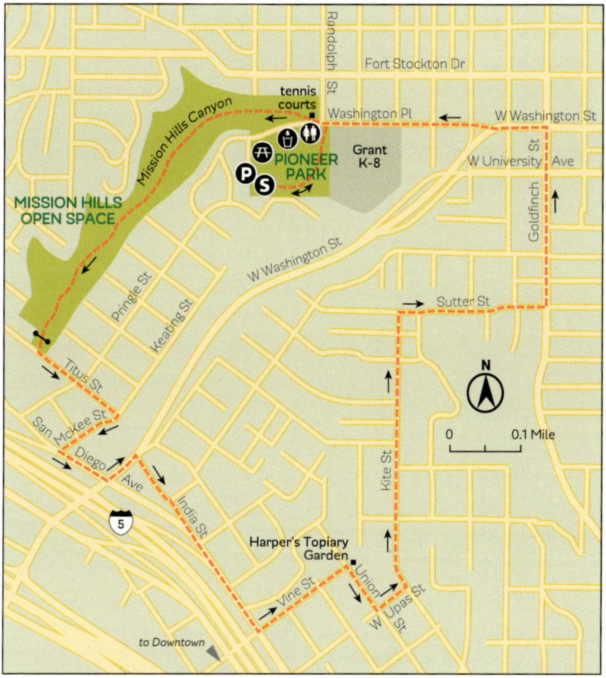

with low-impact check dam structures and restoring natural trees and shrubs.

Exit the Mission Hills Canyon and turn left on Titus Street, following the sidewalk uphill. At the intersection with Keating Street and McKee Street, turn right. Follow McKee Street downhill before turning left on San Diego Avenue. At the intersection with West Washington Street, use the crosswalk to cross the street and turn left. Cross India Street and turn right. Follow India for about 0.3 mile, passing through a bustling hub for international food and drink. Cross Vine Street and turn left. Walk uphill three blocks and turn right on Union Street. Here, pause to gaze across the street.

At 3549 Union Street, Harper's Topiary Garden covers the hillside lawn of the Harper family's private residence. A real-life *Edward Scissorhands* garden, it contains more than fifty plant sculptures including a rabbit, whale, caterpillar, rooster, cat, and dragon. All the plants are trimmed by hand. Entering the garden is prohibited, so please admire it from the street or sidewalk.

At the next intersection, turn left on West Upas Street. Follow it for one block before turning left on Kite Street. Follow Kite Street until its intersection with Sutter Street, then turn right. In this section, take in the beautiful homes. Some of the architectural styles found here include Craftsman, Bungalow, Spanish Colonial Revival, and Prairie School style. Turn left on Goldfinch Street, then cross West Washington Street at the crosswalk and turn left. Continue on Washington Place until its intersection with Randolph Street. Turn left to reenter Pioneer Park, following the paved path back to the starting point.

GO FARTHER

Explore another Mission Hills canyon, Allen Canyon, from the intersection of Allen Road and Fort Stockton Drive. This trail connects Mission Hills to Mission Valley.

22 Seven Bridges

DISTANCE: 5.7 miles roundtrip
ELEVATION GAIN: 230 feet
HIGH POINT: 340 feet
DIFFICULTY: Easy to moderate
FITNESS: Walkers, runners, and cyclists
FAMILY-FRIENDLY: Yes; terrain is flat and accessible for strollers and children
DOG-FRIENDLY: Yes, leashed

The Spruce Street Suspension Bridge gently sways.

BIKE-FRIENDLY: Yes, though it is recommended that cyclists dismount on bridges

AMENITIES: Restrooms, picnic tables, benches, water, museums, and restaurants

CONTACT: City of San Diego

GPS: 32.73199°, –117.14599°

BEFORE YOU GO: Start early for better parking and less traffic. This is not a hiking trail. There is no set route or signage; you will use city streets to navigate your way to the seven bridges.

GETTING THERE

Map to: Inez Grant Parker Memorial Rose Garden

Public Transit: Take MTS Bus Route 7 to Park Boulevard and Village Place.

Parking: From Park Boulevard, find free parking on the street directly in front of the Rose Garden or in any of the lots at Balboa Park. The most convenient lot to the trailhead is the one closest to the San Diego Natural History Museum. If you park there, walk to the intersection of Park Boulevard and Village Place and cross the street.

The Seven Bridges urban trail offers up a unique opportunity to visit a blend of historical and current bridges along former streetcar access routes. This 5.7-mile loop packs in some of San Diego's best sights, including Balboa Park and the neighborhoods of Hillcrest, North Park, and Banker's Hill. If you want to take a break or add on to your day, you'll have a variety of eateries, watering holes, and museums to choose from.

GET MOVING

Begin on the east side of Park Boulevard and Village Place at the Inez Grant Parker Memorial Rose Garden. Cross east to west over the first pedestrian bridge, the Park Boulevard Bridge, toward Balboa Park's Bea Evenson Fountain. Continue west down El Prado through the heart of Balboa Park, past various museums, gardens, and the California Tower until you reach the Cabrillo Bridge. This multiple-arched cantilever bridge was built in 1914. It crossed a small lake during the 1915 Panama-California Exposition, but today you will use it to take yourself over State Route 163 and out of Balboa Park via Laurel Street.

Continue west as you enter the Banker's Hill neighborhood before turning right on 1st Avenue to reach the third bridge. The 1st Avenue Bridge was built in 1931 and is the only steel-arch bridge in San Diego. It spans Maple Canyon, and as you walk over it, take a quick peek west for views of the ocean and the Point Loma peninsula.

Keep heading north for two blocks to Quince Street, then turn right, continuing until you arrive at the Quince Street Bridge, a wooden-trestle bridge constructed in 1905 for pedestrian access to the 4th Avenue Trolley Station. This bridge also spans Maple Canyon. As you cross, look down at the hiking trail carved into the canyon below. Once on the other side, turn around and return back over the bridge. Head one block west and make a right onto 2nd Avenue.

The California Tower is illuminated by a historic streetlamp on the Cabrillo Bridge.

When you reach Spruce Street, turn left to arrive at the Spruce Street Suspension Bridge, built in 1912. This iconic and gently swaying bridge passes over Arroyo Canyon. It is a popular selfie spot, so get your camera ready! After you cross, turn right onto Brant Street and follow the road as it turns right into Upas Street and then left into Albatross Street. Make a right onto Walnut Avenue and a left onto 1st Avenue. When you reach University Avenue, turn right and journey through the neighborhood of Hillcrest, where there are many restaurants and shops perfect for break time.

MAPLE CANYON: UNDER THE BRIDGE

Leave the hustle and bustle of the city streets behind and extend your Seven Bridges route with a trip underneath the Quince Street and 1st Avenue Bridges through Maple Canyon. Enter the trail to Maple Canyon at the signed entrance on 3rd Avenue between Quince and Redwood Streets. Follow the set of stairs down to the canyon floor. At the bottom, turn right and follow the broad trail along the creek bed. Do not forget to gaze up as you pass under each bridge.

This trail is particularly lovely in the spring, when it is green and teeming with flowers. Notice the mix of native plants, such as lemonade berry and laurel sumac, and nonnative eucalyptus and palm trees. After about a half mile, you'll reach the end of the trail at West Maple Street. Turn around here and retrace your steps back to your starting point.

Continue until you reach Vermont Street, then turn left to go through the shopping area. Cross over the Vermont Street Bridge into the University Heights neighborhood, pausing to read the bridge's words of inspiration. It was built in 1995 to replace a wooden-trestle bridge dating back to 1916. Continue on Vermont Street and turn right onto Lincoln Avenue. Keep going on Lincoln, past Park Boulevard, then turn right onto Georgia Street, where you will find the last bridge. The concrete Georgia Street Bridge was built in 1914 to connect the neighborhoods of Hillcrest and North Park. After crossing it, turn right onto University Avenue and then make a left onto Park Boulevard, following it back to the starting point at Balboa Park.

GO FARTHER

This route has many options for extending your hike, including exploring one of the canyons below the bridges, such as the mile-long Maple Canyon Trail under the Quince Street and 1st Avenue Bridges or the 0.8-mile Arroyo Canyon under the Spruce Street Suspension Bridge.

23 Balboa Park: Central Mesa

DISTANCE: 2.5 miles roundtrip
ELEVATION GAIN: 70 feet
HIGH POINT: 300 feet
DIFFICULTY: Easy
FITNESS: Walkers and runners
FAMILY-FRIENDLY: Yes
DOG-FRIENDLY: Yes, leashed
BIKE-FRIENDLY: Yes, though there is a staircase and many pedestrians
AMENITIES: Restrooms, picnic tables, benches, water, playground, dog park, museums, and restaurants
CONTACT: City of San Diego
GPS: 32.73133°, –117.15790°
BEFORE YOU GO: Occasionally there are closures for special events. This section is heavily trafficked by locals and tourists alike, so start early for fewer crowds.

GETTING THERE

Map to: Intersection of Balboa Dr. and El Prado, San Diego, CA 92103

Public Transit: Take MTS Bus Route 3 or 120 to the intersection of 5th Avenue and Laurel Street. Walk east on Laurel Street 0.2 mile as it transitions to El Prado, then walk to the intersection of El Prado and Balboa Drive.

Parking: From 6th Avenue, turn onto the one-way Balboa Drive. Find a free parking spot along the street, anywhere near the intersection of Balboa Drive and El Prado.

Balboa Park's Central Mesa is the park's densest portion—and its heart and cultural core—home to museums and gardens. The Central Mesa was the site of the 1915 Panama-California Exposition and the 1935 California-Pacific International Exposition. The chief architect of the 1915 Exposition,

The west gate entrance to Balboa Park's Central Mesa

Bertram Goodhue, used Spanish Colonial Revival architecture as the theme. This delightfully ornate style was meant to evoke the glamorous, artistic, unique culture of romantic cities like Seville and Toledo in Spain, and Guadalajara in Mexico. It is still seen today on many of the permanent park structures, now housing museums. This 2.5-mile route explores key areas of the Central Mesa, centered on El Prado, a half-mile-long paved street partially closed to traffic, and Palm Canyon, a dirt trail through an oasis.

Four hundred and fifty palm trees fill the 2-acre Balboa Park Palm Canyon.

GET MOVING

Begin at the southeast corner of El Prado and Balboa Drive. Walk east on El Prado along the massive aqueduct-style Cabrillo Bridge. Built in 1914, it is the main gateway to Balboa Park, standing 120 feet over the canyon. Pass through the west gate, an interpretation of the official seal of the City of San Diego. Stay along the right side of El Prado to Alcazar Garden, at 0.4 mile. Turn right, climbing a few stairs to the formal garden; admire its flower beds and Moorish-style fountains and tiling. Turn left at the south end of the garden and exit using the gate to the right. Turn left on the sidewalk and use the crosswalk to cross the parking lot. Turn right, then immediately turn left to enter Palm Canyon's wooden boardwalk.

Head down the staircase to the canyon's floor, passing a spectacular Moreton Bay fig tree with a massive root system. Loop through this 2-acre canyon; with 450 planted palm trees, it's a shady, lush tropical oasis. Follow the paved path as it transitions to dirt. After 0.2 mile, turn left at the easy-to-miss junction just before a chain-link fence and head downhill before crossing the bottom of the trail and making a short uphill climb. Watch your footing, as this portion is steep and slippery. At the top, turn left and head north. Rejoin the canyon floor, turning right on the paved path. Ascend the wooden staircase and turn right on the boardwalk. At the sidewalk, turn right. Use the crosswalk at the intersection of Pan American Road West and Pan American Road East to head toward Spreckels Organ Pavilion. Turn right, following the path as it curves around the complex that houses the world's largest pipe organ in an outdoor venue. You can catch a free organ concert every Sunday at 2 PM.

At the Japanese Friendship Garden (home to the annual Cherry Blossom Festival in March), turn right and head back to El Prado, then turn right, following it east. The road is closed to traffic here, so you can walk in the street or under the covered awning. Pass the Fleet Science Center on the right and loop around the Bea Evenson Fountain. Between January and March, this area becomes even more picturesque during the ornamental pear tree bloom, when delicate white blossoms fall like snow. Continue past the San Diego Natural History Museum on the right. At 1.6 miles, cross Village Place and turn right.

Follow the sidewalk for 0.1 mile before turning left to enter the Spanish Village Art Center. Admire the colorful flagstone floor as you walk through the complex of various artists' studios and spaces. Exit into the parking lot, following the painted path on the left. At the green delineator post, turn left, then immediately left again to walk south. Notice the bushes lining the path—they are elephant topiaries, indicating close proximity to the San Diego Zoo.

At 1.9 miles, turn right, following Village Place back to El Prado. To the left, in front of the San Diego Natural History Museum, notice the huge, century-old Moreton Bay fig tree, one of the largest in California. At El Prado, turn right. After about 0.1 mile, turn right, following the path parallel to the lily pond toward the Botanical Building. It underwent structural reconstruction from 2022 to 2024 and is one of the largest lath structures in the world. If it's open, walk through this free arboretum, home to 2100 species of exotic plants. Walk back to El Prado on the other side of the lily pond. Turn right on El Prado, heading west toward the intricately detailed, colorfully tiled California Building and Tower, a San Diego icon and the park's signature building. Follow El Prado over the Cabrillo Bridge back to the start.

GO FARTHER

Balboa Park offers more than 65 miles of trails, with options to visit the park's west and east sides, as well as to walk the perimeter.

BALBOA PARK: A CULTURAL AND HIKING OASIS

The 1200-acre Balboa Park is a cultural oasis, home to museums, gardens, and the San Diego Zoo. The park was established in 1868 when 1400 acres of land were set aside. This land parcel, then known as City Park, sat largely undeveloped until 1892, when botanist, horticulturist, and landscape architect Kate Sessions offered to plant one hundred trees a year within the park—as well as donate trees and shrubs around San Diego—in exchange for 32 acres of land within the park boundary to be used for her commercial nursery. When San Diego hosted the 1915–16 Panama-California Exposition, the park was renamed after Vasco Núñez de Balboa, the Spaniard who first sighted the Pacific Ocean during Spain's exploration of Panama. Development from this and the 1935–36 California-Pacific International Exposition created the infrastructure and architectural landmarks that form the basis of present-day Balboa Park. The park and its historic buildings were declared a National Historic Landmark in 1977.

Geographically, Balboa Park sits on an uplifted marine terrace mesa overlooking downtown San Diego, San Diego Bay, and Coronado. This mesa is etched with canyons filled with native coastal vegetation mixed with exotic species such as palms and eucalyptus. Two north-south canyons—Cabrillo Canyon and Florida Canyon—traverse the park and separate it into three parts.

Balboa Park boasts a whopping 65 miles of trails that differ in length, difficulty, and scenery, with nineteen trails beginning at one of five gateways. A comprehensive system of hiking and biking trails was created in 2008 to introduce users to the lesser-known areas of the park and promote a positive recreation experience. Routes are marked with color-coded numbered signs, though they may be difficult to locate at times. Some of the trails are remote, while others weave in and out of high tourist areas featuring museums and park venues.

The collision of culture, history, and nature makes Balboa Park one of North America's most renowned urban parks—a perfect place to explore, for residents and visitors alike!

24 Balboa Park: West Mesa

DISTANCE: 3.6 miles roundtrip
ELEVATION GAIN: 150 feet
HIGH POINT: 290 feet
DIFFICULTY: Easy to moderate
FITNESS: Hikers, runners, and cyclists
FAMILY-FRIENDLY: Yes
DOG-FRIENDLY: Yes, leashed
BIKE-FRIENDLY: Yes, though there is a staircase
AMENITIES: Restrooms, picnic tables, benches, water, and playground
CONTACT: City of San Diego
GPS: 32.72517°, -117.15870°
BEFORE YOU GO: Occasionally there are closures for special events. There are often unhoused individuals and encampments in the more natural areas of Balboa Park. While we did not feel unsafe at any point, if it makes you uncomfortable, plan to do this trail with a buddy during daylight hours.

GETTING THERE

Map to: Marston Point parking lot, Balboa Dr., San Diego, CA 92101

Public Transit: Take MTS Bus Route 3 or 120 to the intersection of 5th Avenue and Elm Street. Walk one block east to the corner of 6th Avenue and Elm Street. At the signed Marston Point Gateway, climb the stairs to the parking area for Marston Point.

Parking: From 6th Avenue, turn onto El Prado. Take a right on Balboa Drive and follow it 0.4 mile to the large parking lot with a flagpole at Marston Point. Find free parking here.

The West Mesa of Balboa Park is a narrow strip of land extending from 6th Avenue to State Route 163, and from the north to south boundaries of the park. This section is characterized by

Juniper Staircase consists of 98 stone steps built by the California Conservation Corps.

to University Ave
Cypress Ave
Cypress Ave
Marston Canyon
Brookes Ave
163
5th Ave
6th Ave
7th Ave
Marston House
Myrtle Ave
Upas St
Upas St
Upas Street Footbridge
Balboa Dr
Cabrillo Canyon
Richmond St
Zoo Dr
Park Blvd
Trees for Health Garden
Quince St
San Diego Zoo
BALBOA PARK
5th Ave
6th Ave
Balboa Dr
Redwood Circle
Village Pl
San Diego Lawn Bowling Club
Cabrillo Bridge
museums
Laurel St
El Prado
El Prado
Bridle Trail
Juniper St
San Diego Chess Club
Juniper Staircase
5th Ave
6th Ave
Balboa Dr
163
Park Blvd
Marston Point
Fire Alarm Building
N
Elm St
0
0.25 Mile
5
5
to Pacific Ocean
to Downtown

manicured grassy spaces and tree groves; it has been primarily set aside for passive recreation, such as sunbathing and picnicking. There is, however, adventure to be had here. This loop combines pavement and dirt trails to take a walk on the wild west side of SR 163 via the Bridle Trail and explore the little-known finger of Balboa Park, Marston Canyon.

GET MOVING

From Marston Point, take in the view of downtown San Diego just past Interstate 5. Turn right out of the parking lot and follow the shoulder of the one-way Balboa Drive as it loops around past the Fire Alarm Building on the right. At 0.4 mile, follow the paved path on the right, labeled Bridle Trail on maps. After about a tenth of a mile, reach the signed Juniper Staircase on the right. Descend these steep steps, continuing on the Bridle Trail as it winds through the park, parallel to SR 163. At 0.7 mile, turn right at the junction to walk under the 1500-foot-long, 125-foot-high Cabrillo Bridge.

The trail moves through a series of small rolling hills. Although the sight, sound, and smell of the adjacent cars and highway are ever present, remember you are hiking on a hidden parcel of wild land at the urban core of the city. Pass through a dense oak tree canopy, then notice a gap in the trees at the former site of a one-hundred-year-old redwood forest grove. The last of these redwoods were cut down in 2018 after the majority died from lack of water. Go through a tunnel under a bridge at around one mile, then pass an abandoned highway exit ramp on the right. Walk under a grove of eucalyptus trees before a short uphill push to a Y junction.

Turn right and follow the Upas Street Footbridge to cross SR 163 and enter Marston Canyon. Immediately after crossing the bridge, turn left on the dirt trail, moving downhill. Within this canyon, two parallel trails follow a creek bed running from Richmond Street to SR 163. At the bottom of the hill, turn left and follow the trail east, away from the highway and into the peaceful canyon. Move left to cross over the dry creek bed. Steep canyon walls extend up to houses on the left, and the creek bed runs parallel to the trail on the right. Here, coastal sage scrub native plants—such as toyon, Mexican elderberry, black sage, Torrey pines, California sagebrush, and coyote brush—mingle with nonnative and ornamental escapees from neighbors' backyards, including garden nasturtiums, fennel, wild radish, and Chinese elms.

At around 2 miles, turn right at the signpost. Just past the park kiosk, turn right onto a narrow singletrack trail. Cross the wooden footbridge and turn right, paralleling the creek on its opposite side. The trail broadens as it approaches a junction at 2.3 miles. Move left, then right to follow the trail back toward SR 163. Walk uphill and turn right to cross the footbridge. Turn right and climb the steep concrete switchbacks. At the top, follow the trail past one of California's finest examples of the Arts and Crafts Movement, the 1905 Marston House, on the right.

At the junction of Upas Street and 7th Avenue, turn left onto the paved path, walking through the manicured section. At 2.9 miles, follow the pathway left through the Trees for Health Garden, an educational garden with medicinal plants. Pass Redwood Circle and lawn bowling fields before reaching the Cabrillo Bridge at 3.4 miles. Turn right on El Prado, where vibrant purple jacaranda blooms brighten the sky from May to August. Use the crosswalk to cross Balboa Drive, then cross El Prado. Past the statue of Kate Sessions, the "Mother of Balboa Park," join the paved path south. Use the crosswalk to cross Juniper Street and stay left on the sidewalk. Pass the San Diego Chess Club, and follow the path back to the starting point.

GO FARTHER

This route has many options for extending length or duration. Balboa Park offers more than 65 miles of trails, with options to visit the park's central and east sides, as well as to walk the perimeter.

25 Florida Canyon

DISTANCE: 3 miles roundtrip
ELEVATION GAIN: 170 feet
HIGH POINT: 280 feet
DIFFICULTY: Easy to moderate
FITNESS: Hikers, runners, and cyclists
FAMILY-FRIENDLY: Yes
DOG-FRIENDLY: Yes, leashed
BIKE-FRIENDLY: Yes; popular place for mountain biking
AMENITIES: Restrooms, picnic tables, and water
CONTACT: City of San Diego
GPS: 32.73905°, -117.14243°
BEFORE YOU GO: Trails are popular with mountain bikers; take caution in the sections of singletrack trail.

GETTING THERE

Map to: 2201 Morley Field Dr., San Diego, CA 92104

Public Transit: Take MTS Bus Route 7 to the intersection of Park Boulevard and Zoo Drive. Continue east on Morley Field Drive for 0.4 mile. Turn right into the parking area for Morley Field Sports Complex, then take an immediate right into the parking area just west of the tennis courts.

Parking: From Texas Street, turn right into the parking lot for the Morley Field Sports Complex. Turn left into the parking area just west of the tennis courts. Find free parking in this lot.

Balboa Park's East Mesa is bordered by Florida Canyon to the west, 28th Street to the east, Upas Street to the north, and Russ Boulevard to the south. It is the park's sports and recreational hub, and its trail system was the birthplace of the Canyoneers program, which has offered free guided hikes, led by volunteer naturalists to educate the public through direct contact, since 1973.

Florida Canyon has remained wild despite many threats, including part of it being used as a city garbage dump and

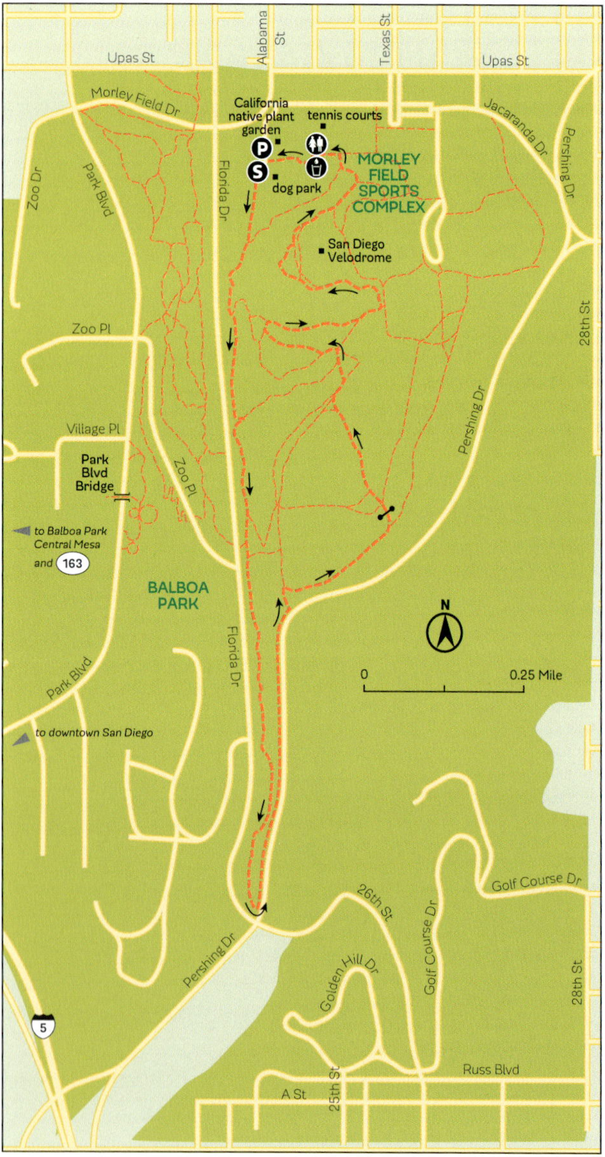
Upas St
Alabama St
Texas St
Upas St
Morley Field Dr
California native plant garden
tennis courts
Jacaranda Dr
Pershing Dr
MORLEY FIELD SPORTS COMPLEX
dog park
Zoo Dr
Park Blvd
Florida Dr
San Diego Velodrome
Zoo Pl
28th St
Pershing Dr
Village Pl
Park Blvd Bridge
Zoo Pl
to Balboa Park Central Mesa and 163
BALBOA PARK
Florida Dr
N
0
0.25 Mile
Park Blvd
to downtown San Diego
Golf Course Dr
26th St
Pershing Dr
Golden Hill Dr
Golf Course Dr
28th St
5
Russ Blvd
A St
25th St

Colorful blooms on coast prickly pear cacti

a naval hospital, failed plans to build a large parking lot, and fires more than four decades ago that greatly diminished the dense, diverse flora. The large trail system pieces together old road segments and footpaths on the east and west sides of Florida Canyon, bisected at the bottom by Florida Drive. This 3-mile loop focuses on trails on the east side of the canyon, minimizing contact with roadways.

GET MOVING

Begin from the parking area just west of the tennis courts off Morley Field Drive. There is a small California native plant demonstration garden adjacent to the parking lot; take an optional stroll here prior to beginning the hike to become familiar with some of the flora you may find along the trail. Walk south across the off-leash dog area until you reach the signed entrance for Florida Canyon Nature Trails. Enter the trail and begin the gentle descent toward the canyon's bottom. Florida Canyon is particularly beautiful during spring, but if you watch closely, there are year-round opportunities to observe the delicate hues of its vegetation—the

A sea of invasive crown daisy in Florida Canyon

jade-green leaves of the manzanita, the flowering yellow tarweed, the silvery-green white sage, and the cream-colored blossoms of the laurel sumac. Though there will be various trails leading up to the mesa top and down to the road, follow the trail running parallel to Florida Drive for a little over a mile, until the intersection of Florida and Pershing Drives.

Take a sharp left turn and follow the trail as it narrows and moves uphill, running parallel to Pershing Drive for about a half mile. At 1.7 miles, stay on the trail as it moves left, away from Pershing. Reach the top of the plateau and turn right onto the wide, flat trail. This section is an excellent place to run laps. In the spring after rain, this part of Florida Canyon is often a sea of gold, due to the attractive, but aggressively weedy, crown daisy. At 1.9 miles, just before the metal gate, turn left and follow the trail as it moves north. At 2.2 miles, turn right on the wide trail, followed by an immediate left, a quick right to move uphill, and then another left to follow the trail west. To the left, there are views of downtown San Diego and the San Diego–Coronado Bridge. Straight ahead, Balboa Park's Central Mesa is visible. Continue following the contour (north, east, north) of the canyon's mesa top until arriving at the back of the velodrome at 2.6 miles.

Turn left on the trail after the No Parking sign. Hike through a huge stand of coast prickly pear cacti bursting with colorful blooms during the spring and early summer. Keep an eye out for birds here, including black phoebes, red-tailed hawks, spotted towhees, hummingbirds, bushtits, and wrentits. Curve around the velodrome. At 2.9 miles, reach the sports complex portion and turn left on the paved path. Just before a park signpost, leave the pavement and follow a faint dirt trail on the left. Walk toward the tennis courts before turning left again, toward a grove of eucalyptus. Follow the wide trail through a nature exploration area, parcourse, and dog park before reaching the starting point.

GO FARTHER

Add on to your trip by visiting the west side of Florida Canyon and additional areas of the East Mesa, such as Golden Hill and the Bennington Memorial Oak Grove.

CANYONLANDS

San Diego is home to more than 150 canyons. Thanks to them, 81 percent of San Diego's 1.4 million residents live within a ten-minute walk of a park or green space. As the population has grown, the flat land across San Diego has been increasingly developed, and these steep, inaccessible canyons have often been left untouched.

Canyons provide important benefits for people, plants, and animals. In fact, San Diego's canyons are home to eighty-five rare, threatened, and endangered species. They serve as important wildlife corridors for animals to safely move through urban spaces they would not otherwise be able to traverse. Canyons absorb and filter stormwater runoff, naturally combating flooding and pollution. Additionally, canyons provide much-needed recreational space.

26 Switzer and Juniper Canyons

DISTANCE: 1.8 miles roundtrip
ELEVATION GAIN: 210 feet
HIGH POINT: 320 feet
DIFFICULTY: Easy
FITNESS: Hikers, runners, and cyclists
FAMILY-FRIENDLY: Yes
DOG-FRIENDLY: Yes, leashed
BIKE-FRIENDLY: Yes
AMENITIES: None
CONTACT: City of San Diego
GPS: 32.73339°, -117.12838°
BEFORE YOU GO: Limited street parking, so public transit or carpooling is recommended.

GETTING THERE

Map to: Intersection of Burlingame Dr. and San Marcos Ave.
Public Transit: Take MTS Bus Route 2 to 30th and Juniper Streets, then walk one block north to Kalmia Street. Turn right onto Kalmia, then after a block, turn left onto San Marcos Avenue, following it as it curves east. At the intersection with Burlingame Drive, turn left; the trailhead is at the end of the road.
Parking: Limited street parking is available around the trailhead, near the corner of Burlingame Drive and San Marcos Avenue.

This hike weaves through two separate canyons in the southern part of North Park. As an added bonus, you can explore the historic Burlingame district and view the exteriors of a wide collection of early-century Craftsman and Spanish Colonial Revival bungalows as you hike between the canyons.

GET MOVING

From the northern end of Burlingame Drive, you can follow the closed road down to the canyon floor or take the side

Switzer Canyon is tucked into the North Park neighborhood.

trail to the kiosk. The trail will quickly make a turn toward the northeast. Before you make this turn, notice a small tunnel passing under 30th Street. This colorfully spray-painted tunnel exits into West Switzer Canyon; the very bold and adventurous could crouch down and pass through, but we will ignore this option and stay in East Switzer Canyon. The trail works its way past eucalyptus and palm trees, crossing over the usually dry drainage. After about 0.4 mile, staying to the right at the junctions, make a short climb out of the canyon onto

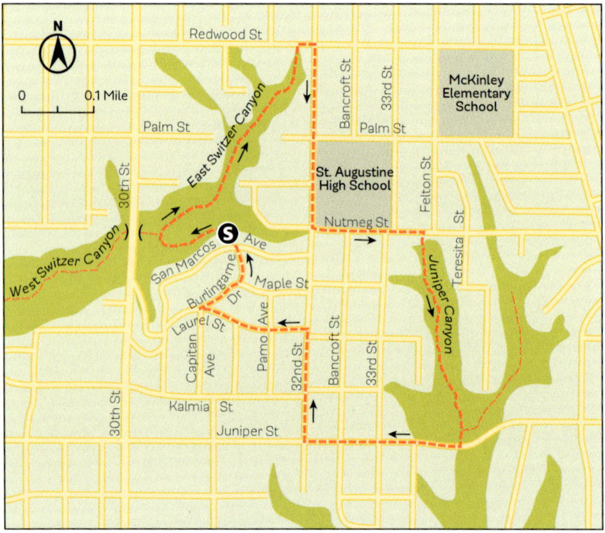

Redwood Street. Turn right on Redwood and then, at the corner, make a right onto 32nd Street. Walk south along 32nd, past St. Augustine High School to Nutmeg Street.

Turn left onto Nutmeg, and the trailhead to Juniper Canyon will be on your right in three blocks. Enter the canyon from the north end and notice a kiosk just past two large trees. While the section of trail in this canyon is short, about 0.3 mile from end to end, directional signs indicate the distance to various entry and exit points. The trail transitions from dirt to a short section of smooth river stones, then back to dirt. Just before you reach the exit from the canyon onto Juniper Street, a spur trail leads off to the northeast. Feel free to explore it, but this trail unfortunately does not allow passage back to the surface streets.

Turn right on Juniper Street, head west for three blocks back to 32nd Street, and turn right (north). You might notice something different between the two sides of the street—the sidewalks on the west are pink in color, while the east side is the traditional gray. The pink concrete was used when this section of the city was developed by the original builders and now serves as an unofficial boundary to the historical Burlingame district.

As you pass the homes here, note that some have markers noting their historical status. Turn left onto Laurel Street and follow it for three blocks to Burlingame Drive. Turn right at this intersection and follow it back to where you started.

GO FARTHER

If architectural design is something that interests you, continue strolling through the neighborhood to view other homes. The local preservation society leads tours of the area as well.

27 City Heights Canyons Loop

DISTANCE: 3.8 miles roundtrip
ELEVATION GAIN: 240 feet
HIGH POINT: 340 feet
DIFFICULTY: Moderate
FITNESS: Hikers and runners
FAMILY-FRIENDLY: Yes
DOG-FRIENDLY: Yes, leashed
BIKE-FRIENDLY: No
AMENITIES: Restrooms, picnic tables, benches, water, and playgrounds
CONTACT: San Diego Canyonlands, City of San Diego
GPS: 32.73251°, −117.10797°
BEFORE YOU GO: Make sure you have a map on hand; though there is ample signage, this trail system involves walking on city streets in order to link the canyons.

A bridge in Hollywood Canyon along the City Heights Canyon Loop Trail

GETTING THERE

Map to: Azalea Recreation Center, 2596 Violet St., San Diego, CA 92105

Public Transit: Take MTS Bus Route 965 to Pepper Drive and Tulip Street. Walk on Azalea Park's pathway to the recreation center building.

Parking: From Poplar Street, curve onto Violet Street. Remain on Violet until you see the recreation center ahead. Free parking is available in the lot.

The City Heights Canyons Loop is a 3.8-mile section of trails connecting four canyons (Swan, Manzanita, Hollywood, and Olivia Canyons) via "butterfly corridors," urban areas that link the canyons and consist of city streets, pocket parks, murals, and native plant gardens. This remarkable trail system opened in 2017 and helped transform 90 acres of degraded, inaccessible urban open space into a safe recreational and transit resource for the eighty thousand residents of the densely populated, diverse City Heights neighborhood.

Dedicated volunteers and organizations, including the Friends of Canyons groups and San Diego Canyonlands, spent years building bridges and stairways, cleaning trash, and eradicating invasive plants to restore the canyons back to their native habitat. The best time of year to visit here is spring, when native plants are blooming.

GET MOVING

Begin your journey at the Azalea Recreation Center. Follow the paved path to the left of the building. Turn right and walk between the playground and basketball court, continuing across a grassy field until you reach the fence line. Turn left, following a faint trail downhill. At the sign indicating Manzanita Canyon, enter the trail and continue downhill. You will see and hear cars whizzing by on busy Interstates 15 and 805. Follow the stairs to the canyon's rocky bottom at 0.3 mile. There

are various exits, but continue straight for the length of the canyon. It tends to be quite rocky, so look for the best path as you move.

After about a mile, exit past the white gate. Continue straight a short distance to a footbridge on the right. Turn right, crossing the bridge and moving uphill. At the top, the Manzanita Gathering Place will be to the right, offering benches and shade. Continue on the trail and turn right on 43rd Street, then left on Thorn Street, crossing Fairmount Avenue.

Thorn Street meets Olivia Canyon past its intersection with Menlo Avenue. Find the trailhead to Olivia Canyon on the left—a narrow path peeking out between a tree and metal fencing. Follow the trail downhill and, at 1.7 miles, cross the creek bed and use the stairs to regain the trail. Turn right at the sign for Quince Street Trail. Follow it about a quarter mile until you reach a gate with an exit to Euclid Avenue on the left. Do not exit through the gate, but instead turn right here,

This mural was created in 2024 by artist Shayne Oseguera, park rangers, and Swan Canyon community members.

following signs for Quince Street Trail and passing Nate's Garden Grill and City Nursery. Travel uphill, then downhill, until you reach the sandy canyon floor at 2.1 miles. Cross it and follow the trail to the right to move uphill.

At the end of the trail, turn right on the sidewalk at Quince Street. Turn left on Menlo Avenue, then right on Olive Street. Cross 46th Street and enter Swan Canyon using the trail to the right. Follow it downhill using switchbacks and stairs. At the bottom, cross the wooden bridge and continue straight, following the sign for Olive Street Trail.

Climb out of the canyon using the trail interspersed with stairs. At the end of the trail, turn right on Olive Street. When Olive dead-ends into Columbine Street, turn left. Look for the sign for Hollywood Canyon on the right. Follow a grassy trail downhill as it gives way to dirt. Reach a junction with a staircase and turn left, following signs for Violet Street Trail. Continue as the trail moves right and enters Hollywood Park. Walk across it, traveling uphill.

Prior to reaching the restroom, turn right on the Violet Street Trail through a gate in the fence. Follow the corridor between homes as it turns left. Reach Violet Street and turn right. Walk on the sidewalk until Poplar Street. Turn left here and walk back through the park to the starting point.

GO FARTHER

There are additional trail segments within the canyons; this route was developed to minimize backtracking.

OPPOSITE: *The infamous and steep South Fortuna Stairs (Trail 31)*

MISSION TRAILS

28 Cowles Mountain and Pyles Peak

DISTANCE: 5.8 miles roundtrip
ELEVATION GAIN: 1900 feet (825 feet to Cowles Mountain)
HIGH POINT: 1591 feet (Cowles Mountain); 1379 feet (Pyles Peak)
DIFFICULTY: Challenging
FITNESS: Hikers and runners
FAMILY-FRIENDLY: No
DOG-FRIENDLY: Yes, leashed
BIKE-FRIENDLY: No
AMENITIES: Restrooms and water
CONTACT: Mission Trails Regional Park
GPS: 32.80440°, −117.03782°
BEFORE YOU GO: Trail is open twenty-four hours and is a popular full-moon hike.

GETTING THERE

Map to: Cowles Mountain trailhead

Public Transit: Take MTS Bus Route 115 to Jackson Drive and Golfcrest Drive. Head northeast on Golfcrest and cross Navajo Road to find the trailhead on the right.

Parking: The trailhead is located at the corner of Golfcrest Drive and Navajo Road. You can find parking in the small dirt lot or along Golfcrest Drive. Note that there have been break-ins here, so do not leave anything of value in your vehicle.

As the highest point in the city, Cowles Mountain draws many hikers to its accessible summit. Cowles Mountain (pronounced *kohls*) got its name from George A. Cowles, one of San Diego's early prominent ranching pioneers. Its top offers great views of San Diego. If you want a challenge or to escape the crowds, continue your adventure by hiking over to Pyles Peak, named after a local family.

Hiking to the summit of Cowles Mountain is a rite of passage for many San Diego hikers. The climb offers great

Summit marker atop Pyles Peak

views of the city (assuming the marine layer has not made an appearance) and a great workout. These two factors make the trail a bit more crowded than some people prefer.

GET MOVING

The ascent to Cowles Mountain begins right from the trailhead, so make sure you are ready to go from the beginning. The climb is, for the most part, a constant one, so take your time as you work your way up. There is no shade on this hike, so make sure you have enough water and sun protection before you go. The first part of the trail is mostly dirt, but it

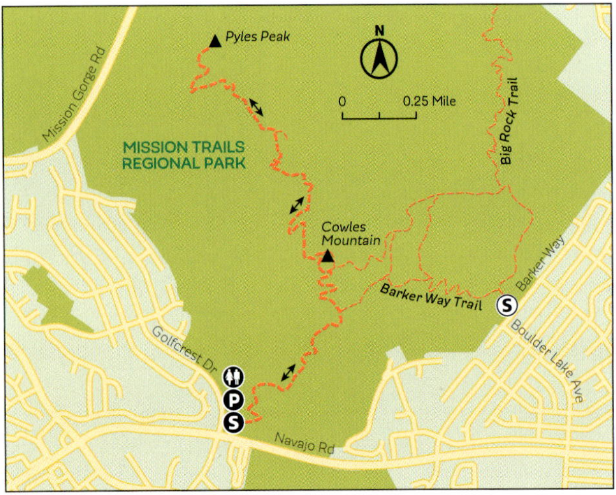

transitions into rockier terrain later. If you are hiking after dark, a good light source is critical to avoid a misstep.

At just under 1 mile, reach the junction that connects to the Barker Way Trail, but stay to the left and continue climbing. Off to the south, you will have a good view of Lake Murray. From here, it is 0.5 mile more to the summit. Soon, come to a series of switchbacks just before the actual summit. Once the switchbacks are done, the summit comes into view. Like all five peaks in Mission Trails, there is a prominent marker here, along with informational panels and a semi-destroyed benchmark. Rest here, or take the wooden stairs to the north, following the service road to the east for a short bit to a usually quieter and less crowded spot.

After your break, it is time to head to Pyles Peak. Continue west along the service road toward the towers until you see a sign for Pyles Peak on the left. Almost immediately, you'll leave the noise and crowds behind. The trail descends from the summit of Cowles toward a rolling saddle before making its way back up to the Pyles summit. All told, you'll lose about 350 feet of elevation before climbing back up and over a small bump en route to the final climb up Pyles Peak.

Come to a small wooden fence overlook after about 1.25 miles, where you'll start the last 0.25 mile to the summit. After gaining another 225 feet, reach the top of Pyles Peak. From here you can see Kwaay Paay and the Fortunas to the northwest. Behind you loom the towers atop Cowles Mountain, along with the climb back up to them. To the east, you should be able to see El Cajon Mountain and even Cuyamaca Peak behind it. Once you are done enjoying the view, and hopefully the peacefulness of this summit, return back along the same route.

GO FARTHER

If you are looking to avoid the crowds that you will find hiking Cowles Mountain from the Golfcrest trailhead, try the alternative trailheads from Barker Way or Big Rock Park.

29 Kwaay Paay Peak

DISTANCE: 2.9 miles roundtrip
ELEVATION GAIN: 870 feet
HIGH POINT: 1190 feet
DIFFICULTY: Challenging
FITNESS: Hikers
FAMILY-FRIENDLY: No
DOG-FRIENDLY: Yes, leashed
BIKE-FRIENDLY: No
AMENITIES: Restrooms and water at Kumeyaay Lake Campground
CONTACT: Mission Trails Regional Park
GPS: 32.84030°, –117.03702°
BEFORE YOU GO: Mission Trails Regional Park closes to vehicles at 5 PM during the winter months, and at 7 PM during daylight savings time.

The short and steep trail to Kwaay Paay Peak

GETTING THERE

Map to: Mission Trails, Kwaay Paay Peak

Public Transit: Take MTS Bus 834 to Mission Gorge Road and West Hills Parkway. Walk west along Mission Gorge Road, then take a slight right onto Father Junípero Serra Trail to the dirt parking lot.

Parking: Parking is available in a dirt lot at the corner of Father Junípero Serra Trail and Bushy Hill Drive. If the gate into Mission Trails is open, proceed along Father Junípero Serra Trail and park along the side of the road closer to either trailhead for Kwaay Paay Peak.

Kwaay Paay—meaning "chief" in the language of the Kumeyaay people, who called the area home for thousands of years—stands alone on the southeast side of Mission Gorge. If you're looking for a good workout, this hike can't be beat.

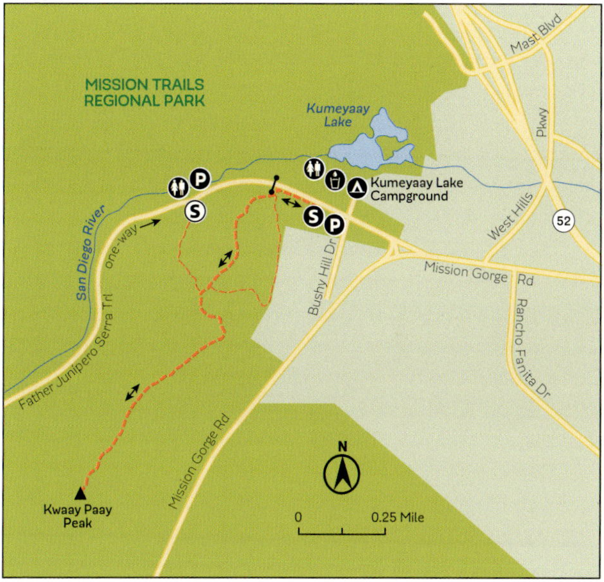

GET MOVING

From the dirt lot, walk west for about 0.2 mile along the road until you reach the trailhead. A sign along the south side of the road marks the start. The trail quickly forks—take the trail to your right and begin your first climb. After cresting a small bump, descend to a small saddle. To your left, a trail that descends east can be used as an alternate route on your return from the summit. Just past this junction, notice a trail to the right, which descends to the northwest and joins the Father Junípero Serra Trail near the Old Mission Dam.

Continue straight past both of these side trails and begin the real climb to the summit. The trail is devoid of switchbacks, so you'll approach the summit directly. To the west lie the summits of North and South Fortuna (see Trails 30 and 31, respectively). To the south, you should be able to spy Pyles Peak and the antenna-covered Cowles Mountain (the high point of the city of San Diego) from time to time. Wooden stairs occasionally help ease the effort. This is a hike where trekking poles are welcomed. Soon, all this effort is rewarded with views from the summit. A wooden fence guards the surrounding vegetation, so be respectful and do not go beyond it. A summit monument offers information about the peak. On a clear day, the summit offers sweeping views of downtown San Diego.

After taking a well-earned rest on one of the boulders, return the way you came, taking care on the steeper sections (did we mention using trekking poles?). While descending, you will be rewarded with a nice view to the north of Kumeyaay Lake Campground and the grasslands beyond. If you hike this peak in the spring, wildflowers should surround you along the trail.

GO FARTHER

At the small saddle near the start of the trail, take either of the side trails to turn this hike into an inverted lollipop. There are several other trails in the vicinity, including others in Mission Trails, in particular North Fortuna (Trail 30). Or connect to the nearby Grasslands Loop (Trail 32) via the alternate trailhead.

30 North Fortuna

DISTANCE:	4.4 miles roundtrip
ELEVATION GAIN:	1040 feet
HIGH POINT:	1291 feet
DIFFICULTY:	Challenging
FITNESS:	Hikers
FAMILY-FRIENDLY:	No
DOG-FRIENDLY:	Yes, leashed
BIKE-FRIENDLY:	No
AMENITIES:	Restrooms and water at Kumeyaay Lake Campground
CONTACT:	Mission Trails Regional Park

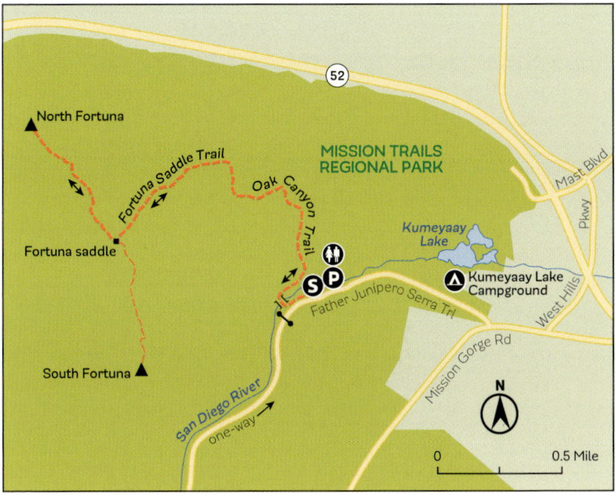

GPS: 32.83973°, –117.04163°

BEFORE YOU GO: Mission Trails Regional Park closes to vehicles at 5 PM during the winter months, and at 7 PM during daylight savings time.

GETTING THERE

Map to: Old Mission Dam

Public Transit: Take MTS Bus 834 to Mission Gorge Road and West Hills Parkway. From there, walk west along Mission Gorge Road, then take a slight right onto Father Junípero Serra Trail to the dirt parking lot.

Parking: Limited parking is available at the Old Mission Dam. If the lot is full, park along Father Junípero Serra Trail.

One of two peaks in the western portion of Mission Trails Regional Park, North Fortuna provides sweeping views of the city. This moderate trail works its way past a seasonal stream before climbing to the summit. If you have ever driven east along State Route 52, you have seen this peak standing just to the south of the freeway.

MISSION TRAILS REGIONAL PARK

The sixth-largest municipally owned park in the United States, and the largest in California, Mission Trails Regional Park covers more than 8000 acres of both developed and natural recreational areas. Originally, this area was used by the Kumeyaay, and evidence of their activity still exists throughout the park. Later, when early European settlers arrived, they constructed a dam across the San Diego River to store water for the nearby Mission San Diego de Alcalá.

During World War II, the area was known as Camp Elliot, a Marine Corps artillery training facility. There are still warning signs posted about unexploded ordnance that might still exist. The park was created in 1974 and offers a wide range of activities, from hiking and biking along its nearly 60 miles of trails to camping at Kumeyaay Lake or boating on Lake Murray. For the more adventurous, Mission Trails is home to the informal 5-Peak Challenge, where participants climb each of the named peaks within the park. More than fifteen thousand climbers completed it before the formal challenge ended in 2020.

The park is also home to a state-of-the-art visitor and interpretive center, located just off Mission Gorge Road. Mission Trails Regional Park closes to vehicles at 5 PM during the winter months, and at 7 PM during daylight savings time, but the park itself is open twenty-four hours.

GET MOVING

Starting from the Old Mission Dam parking lot, head along the trail past the dam. If you have never been here, take some time to explore the dam before continuing. It was built more than two hundred years ago to provide water to Mission San Diego de Alcalá, the first Spanish mission in California. Interpretive panels here offer more information. After crossing the iron bridge over the San Diego River, turn right onto the Oak Canyon Trail. Oak Canyon is a riparian habitat with a seasonal stream during part of the year. Coastal live oaks line the sides of the trail as you head northward. During the spring, look for wildflowers in bloom. There is

The final push to the summit of North Fortuna

almost no shade on this hike, so bring enough water and sun protection.

After about 0.4 mile, a connector trail crosses the canyon to the Grasslands Loop Trail (Trail 32), but continue heading north. In another 0.2 mile, reach another junction with the Grasslands Loop Trail, but stay to your left and continue straight. The trail veers toward the west, and the canyon begins to pass through a rocky gorge. Here, find a few small seasonal waterfalls to enjoy. At 1.2 miles, the trail arrives at the Fortuna Saddle Trail, which is actually a well-defined fire access road that goes straight up to the saddle; be prepared for a steep, steady climb. The road can be slippery due to the soil being mostly decomposed granite, so be mindful of your footing as you work your way up. This is doubly important when you are descending this portion. We can't stress enough the value of a pair of trekking poles here.

Once at the saddle between North and South Fortuna, your destination is a mere 0.4 mile north. The actual summit is hidden behind a small false summit, so don't be disappointed to realize you still have just a bit farther to go. The old metal summit sign has been replaced with a lovely metal-and-concrete marker. Take some time and enjoy the 360-degree views from the summit. To the west is the community of Tierrasanta. To the northwest is Marine Corps Air Station Miramar (former home of "Top Gun" and inspiration for the original movie). During its annual air show, this peak can be crowded with spectators. To the east lie the more challenging peaks in San Diego, like El Cajon Mountain and, in the distance, Cuyamaca Peak.

When you are ready to return, retrace your route down the mountain and through the canyon.

GO FARTHER

There are several options to extend your hike. Once you have reached the Fortuna saddle, continue south and climb to the top of South Fortuna. Another choice is to take one of the two connections onto the Grasslands Loop. This is a great option in the spring when wildflowers may be blooming. There are even more options, but we will leave that up to you: pick up a copy of the park's map and create your own adventure!

31 South Fortuna

DISTANCE:	4.8 miles roundtrip
ELEVATION GAIN:	1180 feet
HIGH POINT:	1094 feet
DIFFICULTY:	Challenging
FITNESS:	Hikers
FAMILY-FRIENDLY:	No
DOG-FRIENDLY:	Yes, leashed
BIKE-FRIENDLY:	No
AMENITIES:	None
CONTACT:	Mission Trails Regional Park
GPS:	32.82537°, -117.07681°
BEFORE YOU GO:	With the lack of shade, this hike is best done either in the cooler months or early morning.

GETTING THERE

Map to: West Fortuna staging area or Mission Trails Clairemont Mesa trailhead

Public Transit: None

Parking: A dirt lot is available at the Mission Trails Clairemont Mesa trailhead. If the lot is full, there is street parking along Clairemont Mesa Boulevard. There have been break-ins here, so do not leave anything of value in the car.

While South Fortuna is the lowest of the five peaks in Mission Trails Regional Park, the unique climb to its summit—and its rewarding views—makes it a very popular hike. This route to South Fortuna connects several trails that crisscross this portion of Mission Trails. We strongly recommend carrying a map to help keep you on track.

GET MOVING

From the parking lot, head east across the metal bridge spanning a small ravine, then go left and up the hill. Soon, locate a trail leading off to the right, and take it down and across

another small ravine. After about 0.3 mile, the trail connects with one of the service roads that crosses the western portion of the park. Turn right onto this road, then make an almost complete U-turn at the next junction to follow another road to the east.

At 0.7 mile, reach the San Diego River Crossing Trail. Stay to the left and continue heading east toward Suycott Wash. About 400 feet from this junction, take the trail to your right down into the wash and enjoy some nice shade from the oaks that line the bottom. For much of the hike, there is no shade, so this section can be a welcome relief on a warm day. It is also a nice point to take a break, as the real climb up South Fortuna is about to begin!

The climb up the east side of South Fortuna

After leaving the wash, the trail turns southward and heads toward the ridgeline to the summit. It is here that you will encounter the infamous South Fortuna Stairs. Wooden railroad ties have been secured into the ground, providing "stairs" to ascend 560 feet over a mere 0.4 mile to the summit. This route is very popular with those looking for exercise, so don't be surprised to see trail runners racing up them. Just climb at your own pace and know a great view will be your reward.

At the top of the stairs, continue to follow the trail for 0.3 mile to the actual South Fortuna summit, which should give you time to recover from the climb before you start snapping your summit selfies. From the top, you will have views of Cowles Mountain and Pyles Peak to the south, and Kwaay Paay Peak to the east. On most days, San Diego and the Pacific Ocean will be visible to the west. Below will be the San Diego River, with the paved Father Junípero Serra Trail running next to it.

Once you have soaked in the views, continue north along the trail leading to the North Fortuna summit (Trail 30). If you are up to it, the summit is about 0.5 mile to the north, with about 370 feet of elevation gain. If you want to save the peak for another day, turn left and head west along the Fortuna Saddle Trail. At 2.9 miles, the trail reaches the Fortuna saddle. From there, the trail descends 0.4 mile and reaches a junction with the Rim Trail. Taking it back to the trailhead is an option, but for this route, stay on the Fortuna Saddle Trail.

At 3.5 miles, come to a junction with the Suycott Valley Trail (you were on a portion of this trail earlier in this hike). Continue heading southwest along the Fortuna Saddle Trail for just over 0.5 mile, then go straight at the junction with the San Diego River Crossing Trail. At 4.1 miles, turn right onto the connector trail from the start of the hike, and soon the metal bridge back to the trailhead will come into view.

GO FARTHER

As you can tell by all the trail junctions, you can take many different routes, depending on what you want to explore.

32 Grasslands Loop

DISTANCE:	2.5 miles roundtrip
ELEVATION GAIN:	120 feet
HIGH POINT:	370 feet
DIFFICULTY:	Easy
FITNESS:	Walkers, hikers, runners, and cyclists
FAMILY-FRIENDLY:	Yes
DOG-FRIENDLY:	Yes, leashed
BIKE-FRIENDLY:	Yes
AMENITIES:	Water, restrooms, picnic tables, and horse corrals
CONTACT:	Mission Trails Regional Park
GPS:	32.84692°, –117.03082°
BEFORE YOU GO:	Mission Trails Regional Park closes to vehicles at 5 PM during the winter months, and at 7 PM during daylight savings time.

The wide trail winds through grasslands habitat.

GETTING THERE

Map to: East Fortuna staging area

Public Transit: None

Parking: Parking is available in several dirt lots at the East Fortuna staging area. There are no side streets nearby that allow parking.

The trailhead and staging area, which took sixteen years to be developed, was finally complete in 2020. It offers parking for forty-seven cars and fifteen horse trailers, twelve picnic sites, and four horse corrals. While the staging area is focused on the equestrian users of Mission Trails Regional Park, all others are welcome. This loop takes you through a section of native

Southern California grasslands. Due to invasive grasses, native grasslands are now a rare sight, but this trail offers you a chance to explore one of the few remaining pockets.

GET MOVING

There are two trailheads from the East Fortuna staging area: the Spring Canyon trailhead, located at the northwest corner of the staging area, near the ranger station, and the North Fortuna Perimeter trailhead, located at the southwest corner. Start from the Spring Canyon trailhead and begin walking west along the wide dirt path. Depending on the time of year, you may see a vernal pool if the winter rains have filled this natural depression. The trail bends southward after about 0.4 mile. Continue hiking southward until you reach the North Fortuna Perimeter Trail.

At the T intersection, turn right, and in about 0.1 mile, reach a four-way junction. Take the Grasslands Crossing Trail to the south for 0.2 mile to reach the Grasslands Loop Trail. You will now be hiking through the heart of the grasslands.

The dominant native grass species here is purple needlegrass (*Stipa pulchra*), a perennial bunchgrass. Closer to some of the wetter areas, you will find deergrass (*Muhlenbergia rigens*). The seeds from these grasses were part of the diet of the Kumeyaay, and the grasses themselves were used for baskets.

Looking to the west, you will see the summits of North and South Fortuna, and directly to the south, Kwaay Paay Peak stands proudly. Continue hiking west for 0.4 mile until the trail reaches another T intersection. If you turn right, you will rejoin the North Fortuna Perimeter Trail. Instead, make a left and continue south along the Grasslands Loop Trail. To your right, notice the trees that line Oak Canyon. At 1.2 miles, a connector trail branches off toward Oak Canyon. Feel free to explore it, as there is another trail that allows you to rejoin the Grasslands Loop. This entire portion of Mission Trails is very well signed, so when you reach a decision point like this, you can reference the signs for additional guidance.

Staying on the Grasslands Loop Trail, pass several interpretive signs explaining more about the grasslands and this ecosystem. Soon, you will see a sign for the Old Mission Dam Overlook spur trail. This 120-foot-long trail will bring you to a bench and a nice view of the dam, constructed by early Spanish settlers to provide water to the nearby Mission Basilica San Diego de Alcalá. After enjoying the views, return to the trail and begin heading eastward. At 1.7 miles, locate a sign for the spur to the Grasslands Grinding Rocks. Take this trail to view some *morteros*, or grinding holes, that were used by the Kumeyaay. An interpretive sign gives information about them. Continue back to the main trail and, in 0.2 mile, reach the Grasslands Crossing Trail. An information kiosk and a bench are located here. Turn north and follow the trail for 0.2 mile until you again reach the North Fortuna Perimeter Trail. Turn right and continue due east for 0.4 mile, back to the East Fortuna staging area.

GO FARTHER

This loop can also be done from the south, using either the trailhead west of the Kumeyaay Lake Campground or beginning at the Old Mission Dam and using the Oak Canyon Trail to connect to the Grasslands Loop.

33 Lake Murray

DISTANCE:	5.6 miles roundtrip
ELEVATION GAIN:	90 feet
HIGH POINT:	560 feet
DIFFICULTY:	Easy to moderate
FITNESS:	Walkers, runners, and cyclists
FAMILY-FRIENDLY:	Yes
DOG-FRIENDLY:	Yes, leashed and at least 50 feet away from water
BIKE-FRIENDLY:	Yes
AMENITIES:	Restrooms, picnic tables, benches, water, concession stand, fishing, and boating
CONTACT:	City of San Diego
GPS:	32.78577°, -117.03859°
BEFORE YOU GO:	Open daily sunrise to sunset; gate to parking lot closed and locked at posted time around sunset; closed second Tuesday of each month.

GETTING THERE

Map to: 5540 Kiowa Dr., La Mesa, CA 91942

Public Transit: Take MTS Bus Route 14 to Lake Murray Boulevard and Kiowa Drive. Walk 0.2 mile north on Kiowa Drive to the park's entrance. Enter the park and follow the pathway to the gate for the perimeter service road.

Parking: From Kiowa Drive, enter the park and find free parking at the easternmost lot. Walk a short distance to the yellow gate blocking vehicles from entering the perimeter service road.

The wide, paved path along the shore of Lake Murray

Sparkling views of Lake Murray along the trail

What are commonly referred to as the San Diego city lakes are part of the municipal water supply system that provides drinking water. The public is given supervised access to these impounding reservoirs for a variety of outdoor activities, including fishing, boating, hiking, and picnicking; swimming and wading are prohibited.

Located within the boundaries of Mission Trails Regional Park, Lake Murray is a very popular place for local residents to bike, jog, walk, rollerblade, and picnic. Be aware that you cannot walk all the way around the entire perimeter of the lake; you can walk only to the dam gate and then must return the way you came.

GET MOVING

Begin your route at the yellow gate entrance to the Lake Murray Path. This perimeter service road is closed to automobiles and is paved, smooth, typically wider than five feet, and gentle, with an estimated maximum grade of 3 percent. It is accessible in all different types of weather, from rainy to hot. All these characteristics make it an ideal place for everyone, including new hikers, people recovering from injuries, wheelchair users, and families with strollers.

Enter the gate and take the path past a map and information board to the right. As you walk on the road, you will see various dirt paths along the shoreline and slopes that diverge from and then return to the main paved path, as well as entrances to the surrounding neighborhoods via Baltimore Drive and Murray Park Drive (by Lake Murray Community Park). Feel free to explore at your leisure, then continue on the path.

Not only will you be treated to sparkling lake views for the duration of your journey, but you will also see a variety of native plants typical of the chaparral and coastal sage scrub habitat. Keep an eye out for Cowles Mountain rising out of the east horizon, and watch for birds. Lake Murray is home to more than 140 species—a mix of aquatic fowl (ducks, coots, white pelicans, great blue herons, and nesting ospreys) and large birds (hawks, ravens, and vultures).

After swinging around the four arms of the lake, the publicly accessible part of the road comes to an end just before the Lake Murray Dam, after a little less than three miles of walking. Here, you will find a bull's-eye sign. Give it a tap—every local knows you have not truly completed this trail until you touch it for good luck. Turn around here and retrace your path back to the starting point.

GO FARTHER

Explore additional routes in Mission Trails Regional Park. Circumnavigate the lake using the Lake Murray Path and sidewalks in the neighboring areas of San Carlos, Del Cerro, and La Mesa.

OPPOSITE: *Where to next? You have a lot of choices at Chollas Lake Park (Trail 38).*

New York 2,761 Mi.
Carver Elementary Gate
Japan 5,626 Mi.
College Grove Dr.
Main Lake Area
Canada 1,369 Mi.

EAST

34 Shepherd Canyon Loop

DISTANCE:	3.5 miles roundtrip
ELEVATION GAIN:	300 feet
HIGH POINT:	540 feet
DIFFICULTY:	Easy
FITNESS:	Hikers, runners, and cyclists
FAMILY-FRIENDLY:	Yes
DOG-FRIENDLY:	Yes, leashed
BIKE-FRIENDLY:	Yes
AMENITIES:	None
CONTACT:	City of San Diego
GPS:	32.83343°, -117.10117°

GETTING THERE

Map to: Intersection of Santo Rd. and Antigua Blvd.
Public Transit: Take MTS Bus Route 25 to Clairemont Mesa Boulevard and Santo Road. Walk about 0.2 mile north to the East Shepherd Canyon trailhead.
Parking: While the trailhead is at the corner of Santo Road and Antigua Boulevard, on-street parking is located west of Santo Road on Tortuga Court.

This gentle, semi-shaded loop takes you through canyons and green spaces in the northern portion of the community of Tierrasanta. This neighborhood was first created in 1971 on land formerly known as Camp Elliot. During World War II, Camp Elliot was a Marine Corps training facility, and the areas of Tierrasanta and Mission Trails Regional Park were used for artillery training. While the government did clear the area of any unexploded ordnance, warnings are still posted, cautioning people that some might be undiscovered and not to touch any they may find. This hike links segments of Shepherd Canyon to create a long urban hike.

GET MOVING

On the southeast corner of Santo Road and Antigua Boulevard, find the dirt path leading into the shallow canyon, as well as an information kiosk. This section is also known as the Shepherd Canyon Native Plant Trail. Back in 2014, Girl Scout Troop 3278 created and installed a series of plaques along this section of the East Shepherd Canyon Trail to identify the native plants found here. Originally, these plaques were painted black with silver lettering, but the passage of time has removed the paint, making them a bit harder to read.

The trail meanders east, passing the occasionally flowing creek, with intermittent shade from eucalyptus trees. After 0.7 mile, come to a sign for Dishwasher Pond. Take the very short trail to a couple of nice benches that provide a lovely view back along the canyon you just hiked through. The pond itself is mostly obscured in reeds and brush but still provides

Shepherd Canyon in Tierrasanta

a nice spot for a quick break. Rejoin the main trail and continue east until it makes a short climb out of the canyon and onto Via Valarta. Turn left at the road, following it north past the church, then use the crosswalk at Via Playa de Cortes to access the next section of the loop. Find the trail heading northeast, passing through a wide-open green space. Occasional side trails link to the surrounding neighborhoods, but continue eastward along the main trail. There isn't as much shade for this portion, so a good hat and sunscreen are recommended.

At 1.8 miles, the trail crosses into the western edge of Mission Trails Regional Park. Instead of continuing into Mission

Trails, turn left, staying on the wide San Diego River Crossing Trail. Condos will be to your left, and after 0.3 mile, you will reach the North Fortuna Perimeter trailhead. Ignoring that trail, turn left and follow the trail that parallels the condos to the south and State Route 52 to the north. When you reach Portobelo Drive, carefully cross the street, as there is no crosswalk, and walk a short distance west to Shepherd Canyon Mini Park. Take the North Shepherd Canyon Trail and follow it to Villarrica Way. Use caution crossing Villarrica, then continue southwest for 0.5 mile to Antigua Boulevard. Turn right and follow the trail back to where you started.

GO FARTHER

If you look across Santo Road at the start of this hike, you might spy a trail sign for West Shepherd Canyon. It is possible to keep exploring the area by taking that trail. However, after 0.3 mile, it ends at Clairemont Mesa Boulevard.

35 Rancho Mission Canyon

DISTANCE: 3 miles; 1 mile; 1.8 miles
ELEVATION GAIN: 200 feet; 100 feet; 220 feet
HIGH POINT: 530 feet; 400 feet; 540 feet
DIFFICULTY: Moderate
FITNESS: Hikers, runners, and cyclists
FAMILY-FRIENDLY: Yes
DOG-FRIENDLY: Yes, leashed
BIKE-FRIENDLY: Yes
AMENITIES: Playground
CONTACT: City of San Diego
GPS: 32.80584°, –117.06567°
BEFORE YOU GO: Middle Rancho Mission Canyon's trail surface is a mix of dirt and a streambed. The Upper and Lower Canyons are dirt-only trails.

GETTING THERE

Map to: Rancho Mission Canyon Park
Public Transit: None
Parking: A parking lot is available off Margerum Avenue.

Located just south of Mission Trails Regional Park is Rancho Mission Canyon. From a small neighborhood park, three canyons can be hiked from a single trailhead, making this a unique adventure. Each route begins from the same parking lot. However, there is a short connector trail between the Upper and Middle Rancho Mission Canyon Trails.

GET MOVING

This hike is different from the other hikes in this book: as instead of an out-and-back or a loop route, this is a hub-and-spoke hike. From the same trailhead, the hike will travel along a spoke—in this case, one of the canyons—then return back to the trailhead, which is the hub. You can choose to explore one, two, or all three of the canyons, and in any order you would like.

UPPER RANCHO MISSION CANYON

From the parking lot, take the dirt trail to the kiosk, then follow the stairs up toward the playground. Walk around the playground to the eastern side to locate the trailhead. The trail climbs a small hill and turns northward. After 0.1 mile from the playground, a connector trail to the Middle Rancho Mission Canyon comes in to the right. Stay straight here, and continue to another kiosk and a trail to your left, which leads to the Larchwood Avenue trailhead. Take the trail to your right and continue climbing along the hillside through the chaparral. The trail will arch around the canyon, mostly following the contour of the hill.

When the trail opens up to the north, you will have a great view of Mission Trails Regional Park, including all five named

Chaparral-lined trail in Rancho Mission Canyon in San Carlos

peaks in the park. At 1.5 miles, the trail ends at Hemingway Drive. Retrace your route almost to the start, until the junction past the first kiosk. If you are planning to also hike the Middle Rancho Mission Canyon Trail, follow the trail to your left and take it down the hill. If you're ready to be finished, stay straight and return to where you started.

MIDDLE RANCHO MISSION CANYON

From the parking lot, follow the trail heading east to the kiosk. After 0.1 mile, notice a trail to your right. This leads to Lower

Rancho Mission Canyon Trail. For now, continue straight. In about 300 feet, a trail comes in from the left that connects to the Upper Rancho Mission Canyon Trail. If you are coming from that trail, this is the connecting path. This trail passes through a more well-defined canyon, gradually making its way up. The chaparral is denser through here, and more trees line the trail. A portion follows a streambed for a short while, and if the water is flowing through the drainage, you might hear it.

After 0.5 mile, make a short climb to exit the canyon onto Cabaret Street. Take in a good view of the canyon, then return back the way you came. In 0.4 mile from Cabaret Street, reach the Lower Rancho Mission Canyon Trail junction that you passed earlier. If you'd like to continue hiking, turn left to reach the lower canyon section. Or, if you're ready to be done, stay straight to return to the start.

LOWER RANCHO MISSION CANYON

Starting again from the parking lot, follow the same trail east that takes you to the Middle Rancho Mission Canyon Trail. After 0.1 mile, take the trail to your right. It quickly drops down to the canyon floor and crosses the usually dry stream. A small bridge can help you cross if water is flowing. Follow a series of switchbacks to assist your climb out of the canyon. The turns on this trail have been built up by mountain bikers for their descents, so be mindful and watch for them passing by.

At the top of the hill, the trail eases up as it passes behind several houses before returning to more natural surroundings. In the distance, you should start to see Navajo Road, which will be the turnaround point for this trail. Along the way, pass through chaparral and the occasional cactus. As you draw closer to Navajo Road, notice the large collection of palm trees in the ravine below you. At Navajo Road and the end of the trail, retrace your route to the parking lot.

36 Navajo Canyon

DISTANCE: 2.5 miles roundtrip
ELEVATION GAIN: 250 feet
HIGH POINT: 340 feet
DIFFICULTY: Easy
FITNESS: Hikers, runners, and cyclists
FAMILY-FRIENDLY: Yes
DOG-FRIENDLY: Yes, leashed
BIKE-FRIENDLY: Yes
AMENITIES: None
CONTACT: City of San Diego
GPS: 32.78276°, -117.08632°

Navajo Canyon runs between the Allied Gardens and Del Cerro neighborhoods.

GETTING THERE

Map to: 67 Adobe Falls Rd., San Diego, CA 92120
Public Transit: Take the Green Line Trolley to the Grantville Station, then walk east along Alvarado Canyon Road for about 0.7 mile to the intersection with Adobe Falls Road.
Parking: Parking can usually be found along Adobe Falls Road.

Tucked away near Waring Road and the San Diego State University campus is Navajo Canyon. This short trail leads along a small stream surrounded by plants and wildlife. It is

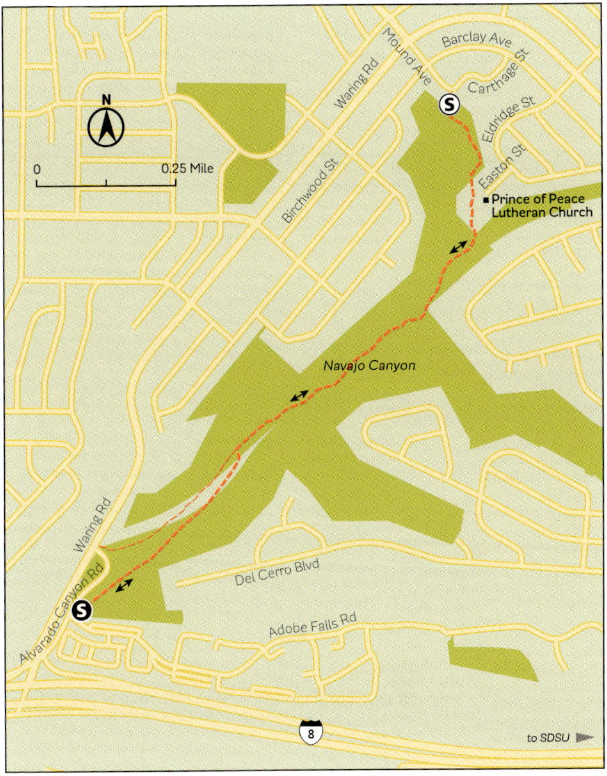

an out-and-back, so you can start either at the Adobe Falls Road trailhead or from Mound Ave.

GET MOVING

Find the trailhead at the corner of Adobe Falls and Alvarado Canyon Roads. The trail heads gently north through the canyon. To your left is a stream that is usually flowing. Sounds of the nearby road quickly fade away, and you are mostly removed from the city. Throughout the canyon, notice the nonnative Mexican fan palms. In addition, look for wild fennel and pampas grass, as well as sage and some other coastal scrub plants.

The trail leaves the flat path you started on and passes through the rocky streambed. A narrow path parallels this section, so you can practice your balance skills along it or walk over the waterworn rocks. Exit this section and return to wide dirt. After the streambed, a few trails appear off to the side, but they are just paths to the utility poles and should be signed as No Access.

Continue north, where you will have a simple water crossing or two to make. Just before the end of the first section, climb a small hill, which ends at the back side of a church's preschool. This is a great spot to turn around and look back down the canyon you just hiked up. The trail continues, so walk past the preschool and the church parking area, then look for a trail sign to the north. This next section is about 0.2 mile each way, but since you have come this far, why not finish the entire route? Dip down into the canyon again before climbing quickly back out. Both this endpoint and the trailhead at the church can be used as alternate starts if you happen to live close to these entry points.

Reach the end of the trail and then simply turn back and retrace your route.

37 Emerald Hills Canyon

DISTANCE: 3 miles roundtrip
ELEVATION GAIN: 240 feet
HIGH POINT: 340 feet
DIFFICULTY: Easy to moderate
FITNESS: Hikers, runners, and cyclists
FAMILY-FRIENDLY: Yes
DOG-FRIENDLY: Yes, leashed

BIKE-FRIENDLY: Yes
AMENITIES: Restrooms, picnic tables, playground, and water
CONTACT: City of San Diego
GPS: 32.72139°, −117.07515°
BEFORE YOU GO: There can be evidence of unhoused encampments as well as trash, alcohol, and drug paraphernalia along this route. Plan to do this trail during daylight hours with a hiking partner.

GETTING THERE

Map to: 5601 Bethune Court, San Diego, CA 92114

Public Transit: Take MTS Bus Route 916 to Bayview Heights Drive and Bayview Heights Place. Walk east on Bayview Heights Drive and then turn right onto Bayview Heights Way. After 0.1 mile, the street becomes Kelton Road. Follow Kelton Road 0.1 mile before turning left onto Bethune Court to arrive at the trailhead.

The magenta flower of the coast cholla

The red stairs down into Emerald Hills Canyon

Parking: From Kelton Road, turn onto Bethune Court and follow it to the large parking lot at Emerald Hills Neighborhood Park. Walk back (west) along Bethune Court to the trailhead on your right.

Chollas Creek is a 32-square-mile natural waterway that courses through park-deficient, historically underserved San Diego communities, from its headwaters in La Mesa and Lemon Grove to San Diego Bay. It was a significant settlement for the Kumeyaay and holds some of the richest cultural, biological, and geological assets in the region. It was also the only city waterway not classified as a regional park; however, in 2021, Chollas Creek Regional Park—a loose collection of small parks, open-space canyons, trails, and other recreational facilities—was created to ensure access for all.

Emerald Hills Canyon is one of the park's open-space canyons, offering about three miles of trails with views of the Coronado Bridge and downtown San Diego. About 80 percent of all city-owned open space in southeastern San Diego is in Emerald Hills.

GET MOVING

Enter the trail through an opening in the fence and walk along the path toward State Route 94. Find a set of red stairs and take them downhill. At the bottom, turn right, following the paved trail as it gently moves downhill. At 0.2 mile, continue as the trail turns right and goes down more stairs, transitioning into a narrow dirt path. You might notice green sewer drains alongside the trail; historically, San Diego's sewer lines were constructed in canyons to take advantage of gravity flow.

Follow the path as it travels east, paralleling the highway and the creek to the left. Though the whoosh of cars is prevalent, listen for the chirping of the various birds that call this canyon home, including the threatened California coastal cactus wren. At 0.7 mile, continue straight at the trail junction, following signs for Federal Boulevard. Follow the trail as it curves to the left 200 feet before coming to an end at a metal gate. Turn around here and retrace your steps uphill to the starting point.

Exit the trail at the fence and cross over Bethune Court. Turn right to follow the sidewalk. Since much of Emerald Hills is hilly, look ahead to see a beautiful view of Coronado Bridge and downtown San Diego. The highest point of Emerald Hills, where transmitter towers for KSDO radio now stand, was once a Kumeyaay burial ground.

When you reach Kelton Road, turn left and walk on the sidewalk past Johnson Elementary School. Use the crosswalk to cross Kelton, and turn right. At 1.6 miles, turn left at the trailhead and follow the trail downhill. Turn right before crossing the creek bed at the canyon's bottom. At the next trail junction, turn right and start an uphill climb. Notice the coastal cholla cacti, alongside other native plants like California buckwheat, lemonade berry, bush monkeyflower, California cudweed, and yerba santa.

At 1.8 miles, turn left at the junction instead of heading toward Zircon Court. Follow the trail as it gently moves downhill for about a tenth of a mile. Turn left at the next junction and take the stairs downhill. Cross the rocky creek bed and move uphill using more stairs. At a sign stating "Ecological Reserve," turn right, following the trail along the fence line and then as it curves to the right.

At 2.1 miles, reach a very rocky, wide creek bed. This is a good place to turn around, or you can cross the creek bed and travel a short distance to the trail's terminus at Elwood Avenue. Retrace your steps back to the trail junction at 2.5

miles and turn left, then immediately turn right. Follow the trail uphill to the exit gate at Zircon Street. Take Zircon to Kelton Road and turn right. Walk on the sidewalk back to the crosswalk, cross Kelton, and turn left. Go right on Bethune Court and follow the road to Emerald Hills Neighborhood Park.

Enter the park's paved path just past the restrooms. Take the quarter-mile loop around the park to return to the parking lot.

38 Chollas Lake

DISTANCE: 2.3 miles roundtrip
ELEVATION GAIN: 220 feet
HIGH POINT: 470 feet
DIFFICULTY: Easy
FITNESS: Walkers, hikers, runners, and cyclists
FAMILY-FRIENDLY: Yes
DOG-FRIENDLY: Yes, leashed
BIKE-FRIENDLY: Yes
AMENITIES: Restrooms, water, and playgrounds
CONTACT: City of San Diego
GPS: 32.73740°, –117.06086°
BEFORE YOU GO: The main gate at the east park entrance, next to the lake, closes 30 minutes before sunset. Other gates close *before* the east gate. Note the closing times if hiking later in the day.

GETTING THERE

Map to: Chollas Lake Park

Public Transit: Take MTS Bus Route 856 to College Avenue and College Grove Drive. Walk west along College Grove Drive for 0.8 mile to the east entrance.

Parking: The main parking area is along the eastern shore of the lake. If this parking area is full, you can park at either Gloria's Mesa (above the southwest corner of the lake) or near the baseball field by the western end of the park.

Reflections on Chollas Lake on a sunny afternoon

Originally built back in 1901 as a water supply source, Chollas Lake was transferred to the San Diego Parks and Recreation Department in 1966. Now the park houses several pavilions, picnic areas, and two playgrounds. One unique feature of the lake is that fishing is only allowed for children under fifteen.

GET MOVING

Starting from the east side of the lake, follow the path counterclockwise around the lakeshore. Just past one of the pavilions, a side trail takes you up the hillside and away from the lake. This trail reconnects at the dam, so the route choice is up to you. If you take the side trail, you will meander through the shaded hillside, getting in some slight elevation. If you stay along the lakeshore, you will pass one of the fishing piers, and probably more of the waterfowl that enjoy the lake (just

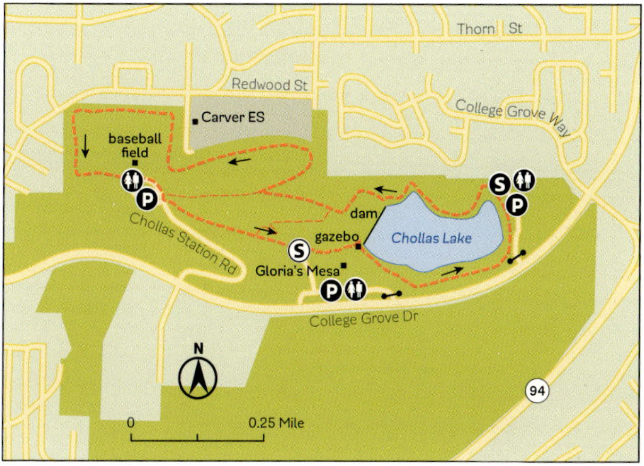

remember that it is illegal to feed them). When you reach the dam, take the trail down from it, through a large eucalyptus grove, and into a wide canyon. If you want to turn back at this point, cross over the dam and follow the shoreline back to your starting point.

At 0.3 mile, reach a junction and take the trail to the right to make a short climb (70 feet of elevation gain) to hike along the top of this mesa. We recommend making the climb, as it provides not only a sweeping view of the canyon floor, but also some good views of downtown San Diego. If you do not feel like making the climb, continue straight until you reach the baseball field. Once atop the mesa, the wide trail hugs the edge, passing an elementary school on the right. The trail loops around the baseball field and then descends back to the canyon floor.

After crossing the parking lot for the baseball field, the trail picks up again on the east side. Continue directly east along the wide dirt road for 0.5 mile back to the dam, or take the singletrack trail to the right, which will gently climb the south side of the canyon for about 0.3 mile toward Gloria's

Mesa. Once at Gloria's Mesa, you will find a small amphitheater, restrooms, and, in the spring, a nice display of wildflowers. When you're done exploring the mesa, follow the trail to the east and back down toward the lake. There is a wooden gazebo at the base of the stairs. Before following the trail along the south side of the lake, take a moment to walk across the dam for a clear view of the lake. The remaining 0.4 mile back to the parking area is under the shade of many eucalyptus trees.

39 Rolando Village Catwalks

DISTANCE: 2.4 miles roundtrip
ELEVATION GAIN: 380 feet
HIGH POINT: 470 feet
DIFFICULTY: Easy to moderate
FITNESS: Walkers and runners
FAMILY-FRIENDLY: Yes, but not stroller-friendly; some stairs might not be suitable for young children
DOG-FRIENDLY: Yes, leashed
BIKE-FRIENDLY: Yes, but not recommended due to stairs
AMENITIES: Restrooms, picnic tables, and water
CONTACT: City of San Diego, City of La Mesa
GPS: 32.75722°, -117.05299°
BEFORE YOU GO: There is no set trail and only limited signage indicating pedestrian passageways with stairs. You will use city streets to navigate. Please be respectful of residents whose homes are next to the stairs and refrain from making excessive noise.

GETTING THERE

Map to: Rolando Park, 6600 Vigo Dr., La Mesa, CA 91942
Public Transit: Take MTS Bus Route 852 to the intersection of University Avenue and Aragon Drive. Head east on University

Paseo del Papagayo catwalk in Rolando Village

Avenue. Turn left onto Alamo Drive and walk 0.1 mile. Take a sharp right onto Vigo Drive. Enter Rolando Park on the left.
Parking: From 70th Street, turn right onto Alamo Way. Follow Alamo Way for 0.5 mile before turning left onto Alamo Drive. Turn left onto Vigo Drive, followed by another left turn into the free parking lot for Rolando Park.

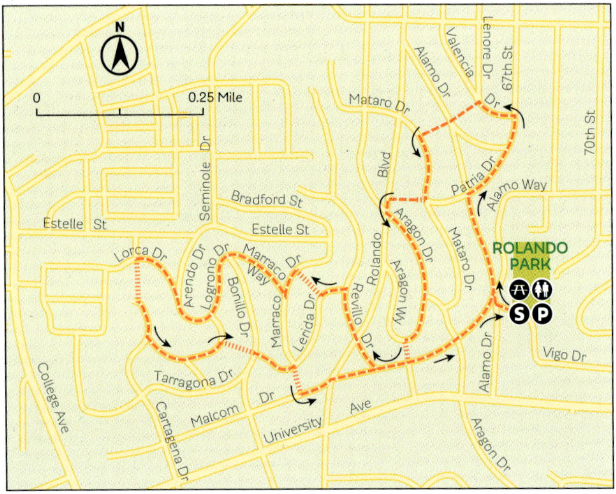

This 2.4-mile butterfly loop around the Rolando Village neighborhood of San Diego highlights eight unique catwalks—pedestrian passageways with ramps and stairs—connecting city streets through a rolling landscape. There are 256 steps across the segments, with more walkways than stairs. Called "Rolando" due to its rolling hills and because Spanish-sounding names were a popular marketing tool at the time, Rolando Village was primarily developed after World War II to accommodate San Diego's rapid growth. These pathways were first constructed when the original sidewalks were laid, connecting tree-lined streets with interesting architecture.

GET MOVING

From Rolando Park in the city of La Mesa, turn right on Vigo Drive. Cross into San Diego, heading north through a whimsical bush tunnel decorated with birdhouses and a Little Free Library. Veer right to cross Alamo Way and continue on Alamo Drive. Turn right on Patria Drive. Head uphill two blocks before turning left on Valencia Drive. One interesting feature of this neighborhood is the acorn-style lampposts found on many streets.

Just before one of these lampposts, near the intersection of Valencia and Lenore Drives (past 4572 Valencia Drive), turn left and enter the first catwalk. Look down to see the Spanish-style tiling indicating the name of the walkway, Paseo del Papagayo (parrot). Unfortunately, some of the signs here and in other catwalks are damaged. This catwalk consists of forty-five steps over four staircases. Head downhill and cross Alamo Drive at the bottom of the catwalk.

Directly across the street, enter the second catwalk, Paseo de la Naranja (orange). This passageway has no steps but heads uphill. At the top, turn left on Mataro Drive. Just before the intersection of Mataro and Patria Drives (past 4510 Mataro Drive), turn right to enter the third catwalk, Paseo del Colibri (hummingbird). Climb a short staircase and a longer ramp. Though most of the vegetation you'll see on this hike will be planted cultivars like succulents, roses, and bougainvillea, in this passageway there is a native plant garden. Watch for plants like California poppies and California buckwheat, especially in the spring. Near the top of the walkway, find a bench perfect for resting, and a canister with catwalk maps.

Exit the catwalk and turn left on Rolando Boulevard. Take another left on Aragon Drive, then veer right on Aragon Way. Just before a yellow fire hydrant (after 4365 Aragon Way), turn left onto the fourth catwalk, Paseo de los Agaves. This catwalk has thirty-seven steps in two stair sections. Head downhill and turn right on Malcolm Drive, then go right on Revillo Drive. Cross Rolando Boulevard and turn left on Lerida Drive. Climb uphill to the fifth catwalk, Paseo de los Coyotes, next to 4410 Lerida Drive. Continue uphill on the thirty steps over four staircases. At the top, turn left on Marraco Drive.

Take a right on Marraco Way, following it to its intersection with Bonillo Drive. Here, Maracco Way changes to Logrono Drive. Follow Logrono to the right when it merges with Lorca Drive, moving left to stay on Lorca. At the intersection of Lorca Drive and Laco Drive, turn left onto the sixth catwalk, Paseo de las Palmas. This catwalk was replaced in 2025 and has thirty-eight wooden and cement steps. Head downhill and go left on Cartagena Drive. Turn left on Rodrigo Drive, then walk uphill past the bungalow-style homes and turn left on Lorca Drive.

Just past 6334 Lorca Drive, go right onto the seventh catwalk, Paseo de los Pinos (pine trees). This steep catwalk is shaded by trees, with sixty-five steps over four staircases. Head downhill and cross Bonillo Drive to continue on Lerida Drive. Where Marraco Drive intersects Lerida (just past 4297 Lerida Drive), turn right onto the eighth catwalk, Paseo del Halćon (hawk). This passageway has thirty-four steps across three staircases. Head downhill and turn left onto Malcolm Drive. Cross Rolando Boulevard and continue on Malcolm Drive. Cross Alamo Drive, then turn right on Vigo Drive to return to the starting point.

40 The Stride: La Mesa Urban Trail

DISTANCE: 5.2 miles roundtrip
ELEVATION GAIN: 120 feet
HIGH POINT: 690 feet
DIFFICULTY: Easy to moderate
FITNESS: Walkers, runners, and cyclists
FAMILY-FRIENDLY: Yes; route can be divided in half
DOG-FRIENDLY: Yes, leashed
BIKE-FRIENDLY: Yes
AMENITIES: Restrooms, picnic tables, playground, benches, and water
CONTACT: City of La Mesa
GPS: 32.78559°, –117.02015°

BEFORE YOU GO: You will use city streets to navigate, with only limited ground markers. Please be respectful of residents whose homes are near the trail, and refrain from making excessive noise.

GETTING THERE

Map to: Jackson Park, 5870 Jackson Dr., La Mesa, CA 91942

Public Transit: Take MTS Bus Route 854 to Lake Murray Boulevard and El Paso Street. From Lake Murray Boulevard, walk to El Paso Street and turn left. Follow El Paso Street for 0.2 mile before turning right on Jackson Drive. Continue on Jackson Drive for 0.2 mile to Jackson Park.

Parking: From Jackson Drive, turn into the parking lot at Jackson Park and find free parking.

The City of La Mesa, "the Jewel of the Hills," launched the City Walks and Urban Trails program as part of their Urban Trails Mobility Action Plan. The intention is to connect the community by establishing a pedestrian urban trail network

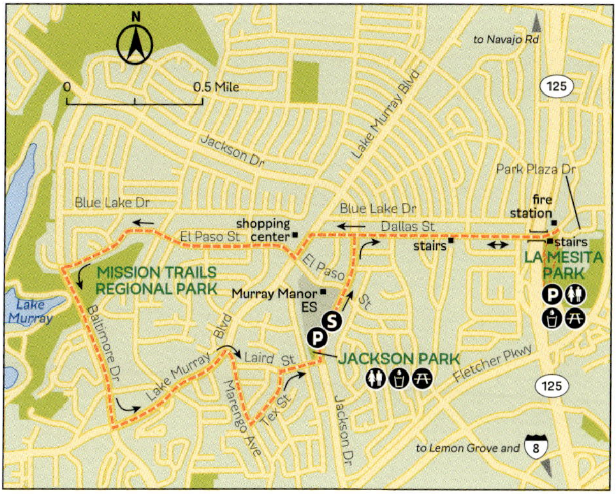

that supports alternative modes of transportation for exercise and mobility. La Mesa is the only city in the County of San Diego actively pursuing the emerging concept of urban trails, which are intended to create branded, signed, identifiable routes connecting key destinations throughout the city.

Currently there are three trails (beginner, intermediate, and advanced), with nineteen additional segments in progress. This route describes the intermediate trail, The Stride, which connects Jackson Park, La Mesita Park, and Lake Murray over about 5 miles, with one hill, mild inclines, and optional stairs.

GET MOVING

From Jackson Park, turn left onto Jackson Drive and follow the sidewalk about a quarter mile to the intersection of El Paso Street. Here, use the crosswalk to safely move to the other side of Jackson Drive. Turn left and continue on Jackson until you reach Dallas Street. Turn right on Dallas and head east toward La Mesita Park. The vegetation along this route matches the slightly drier and warmer climate moving inland from the ocean. Keep your eyes peeled for both native coastal sage scrub species and ornamental heat- and drought-tolerant plants, including laurel sumac, agaves, jade plants, bird-of-paradise, hibiscus, jasmine, roses, crepe myrtle, eucalyptus, jacaranda, mulberry, magnolia, palm, and pine trees.

At 0.8 mile, you will find one of La Mesa's hidden staircases on the right, near a fence with bougainvillea. Take an optional quick detour to check out the passageway, then continue on Dallas Street. Pass over State Route 125 before reaching La Mesita Park at 1.2 miles. Go down the staircase on the right to enter the park. At the bottom of the stairs, turn right and follow the paved path as it loops around the park for about 0.2 mile. When you complete the loop, turn right and follow the paved path uphill to exit the park. At the intersection of Park Plaza Drive and Dallas Street, use the crosswalk to move

A Little Free Library in La Mesa

across Park Plaza Drive, then turn left on Dallas Street and head back west.

As you walk, you may notice silver or green markers embedded into the curb indicating "Urban Walking Trail." These are meant to outline the route. At 2.3 miles, cross over Lake Murray Boulevard and turn left. Walk through the commercial district for one block before turning right on El Paso Street and climbing the steepest hill on the route. As it levels out, take a moment to appreciate how this community developed on top of a mesa (a plateau), lending the city its name. Continue through the landscape, which accommodates both hills and hidden canyons.

When you reach Baltimore Drive, turn left and follow the sidewalk as you enter the Lake Murray basin. Walk past a hidden canyon on the left, a side canyon of Mission Trails

Regional Park. Take a peek at or explore the short loop trail filled with native plants and nonnative palms. On the right, catch a glimpse of Lake Murray sparkling past its neighborhood entrance. Continue on Baltimore Drive, then use the crosswalk to move across Lake Murray Boulevard and turn left.

After about a half mile, just past the bus stop, turn right on Marengo Avenue. Turn left on Tex Street and then right onto Laird Street. At 5.1 miles, turn left on the paved path to enter the shady alcove of Jackson Park. Follow the path through the park back to the starting point.

GO FARTHER

Extend your route by adding on the trail through the side canyon or a portion of the Lake Murray Path (Trail 33).

41 La Mesa Secret Stairs

DISTANCE: 1.5 miles roundtrip
ELEVATION GAIN: 260 feet
HIGH POINT: 830 feet
DIFFICULTY: Moderate
FITNESS: Walkers and runners
FAMILY-FRIENDLY: Yes, but not stroller-friendly; some stairs might not be suitable for young children
DOG-FRIENDLY: Yes, leashed
BIKE-FRIENDLY: Yes, but not recommended due to stairs
AMENITIES: None, but restrooms at La Mesa City Hall
CONTACT: City of La Mesa
GPS: 32.76408°, –117.02016°
BEFORE YOU GO: This is not a hiking trail. There is no set route and only limited signage indicating "Caution: Steps." You will use city streets to navigate. Please be respectful of residents whose homes are next to the stairs and refrain from making excessive noise.

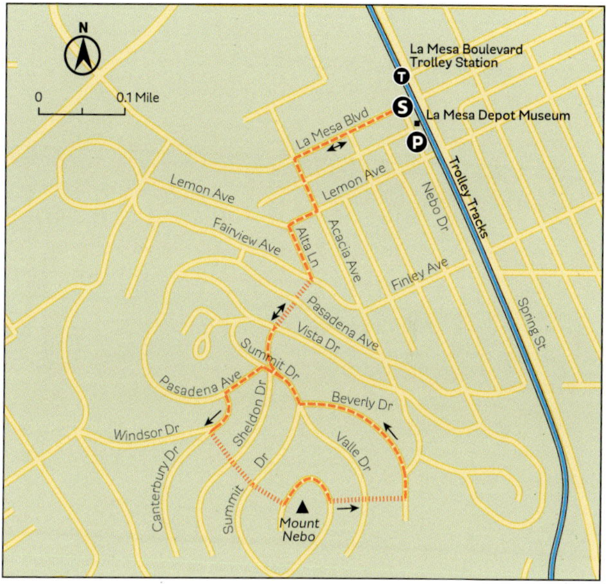

GETTING THERE

Map to: Intersection of La Mesa Blvd. and Nebo Dr., La Mesa, CA 91942

Public Transit: Take the MTS Orange Line Trolley to the La Mesa Boulevard Trolley Station. Exit the station on Spring Street and turn left on La Mesa Boulevard. Cross the street at the intersection of La Mesa Boulevard and Nebo Drive to begin your hike.

Parking: From La Mesa Boulevard, turn onto Nebo Drive and find parking here or at any street parking nearby. Parking is metered near La Mesa Boulevard; free parking begins two blocks away at the intersection of Nebo Drive and Lemon Avenue.

Known as the "secret stairs," the sets of public stairways in the historical Windsor Hills neighborhood of La Mesa offer

Words of inspiration on the La Mesa Secret Stairs

489 steps in seven segments, ascending to 830 feet at the top of Mount Nebo on Summit Drive. Originally built more than a century ago to facilitate foot traffic through adjacent neighborhoods, the stairs are now a popular urban hiking

and exercise destination. It is a great glute workout, and for those preparing for more strenuous mountain climbs, stairs are awesome training. This route covers all 489 steps in a 1.5-mile cherry-stem hike beginning from La Mesa Boulevard. For shorter climbs, you can also start on Summit Drive, Windsor Drive, Canterbury Drive, or Fairview Avenue.

GET MOVING

Start at the intersection of La Mesa Boulevard and Nebo Drive. Take a moment to check out the La Mesa Depot Museum, California's oldest building in its original form and the sole surviving San Diego and Cuyamaca Railway Station in existence. Head west on La Mesa Boulevard, exploring the historic downtown La Mesa area, with its shops and restaurants.

Turn left on Acacia Avenue. Next, turn right onto Lemon Avenue and then left onto Alta Lane. At the end of Alta Lane, cross Fairview Avenue and reach the first series of steps. Ascend the stairs, taking time to admire a variety of colorful planted cultivars, ranging from cacti and succulents to bougainvillea, varieties of flowering ice plant, and nasturtiums. At the top of the stairs, cross Pasadena Avenue and complete the second segment of steps and the paved passageway uphill to Vista Drive. Cross Vista and continue straight on Sheldon Drive. After one block, turn right on Summit Drive, followed by an immediate left onto Pasadena Avenue and a left onto Windsor Drive.

At the intersection of Canterbury Drive and Windsor Drive, you will find a trio of long and steep staircases on the left. Follow these steps up, crossing Sheldon and Summit Drives and then ending at Summit Drive again, when the winding street arrives at the houses adorning the top of Mount Nebo, the peak of the walk. From Mount Nebo, you can see downtown San Diego and the Pacific Ocean to the west and Mount Helix to the east.

After taking in the views and catching your breath, turn left and head east on Summit Drive, circling the road to find a staircase on your left, just past 4250 Summit Drive. Descend one set of stairs to Valle Drive before crossing the street and picking up another set of stairs that will lead you to Beverly Drive. Turn left on Beverly and follow it uphill to the left until you reach Summit Drive.

Turn right on Summit, continuing until it meets with Sheldon Drive to complete the loop. Turn right on Sheldon and follow the cherry stem back down the first segment to repeat the sixty steps to Pasadena Avenue, Fairview Avenue, and the intersection with Alta Lane. Follow Alta and turn right on Lemon Avenue, left on Acacia Avenue, and right on La Mesa Boulevard, which leads back to the starting point.

GO FARTHER

Two out of three of La Mesa's urban walking trails travel on portions of this route: The Stroll, a 1-mile flat beginner route starting from La Mesa Depot Museum, and The Challenge, a 3.5-mile advanced route with hills and a portion of the "secret stairs," starting from Highwood Park. Just 1.5 miles away, check out another set of secret stairs, the rainbow-hued steps painted by artist Magdalena Noriega connecting Stanford Avenue to West Point Avenue.

42 Mount Helix

DISTANCE: 1.7 miles roundtrip
ELEVATION GAIN: 300 feet
HIGH POINT: 1370 feet
DIFFICULTY: Moderate
FITNESS: Hikers, runners, and cyclists
FAMILY-FRIENDLY: Yes

Views from the Yawkey Trail on Mount Helix

DOG-FRIENDLY: Yes, leashed
BIKE-FRIENDLY: Yes
AMENITIES: Restrooms and water
CONTACT: Mount Helix Park Foundation
GPS: 32.77029°, –116.97968°
BEFORE YOU GO: Open 6:30 AM–6:30 PM. Gate below the summit restricts access, even for pedestrians, outside those hours.

GETTING THERE

Map to: 10105 Vivera Dr., La Mesa, CA 91941

Public Transit: None

Parking: From Fuerte Drive, turn onto Mount Helix Drive and follow it 0.2 mile. Turn left onto Vivera Drive. Free parking is

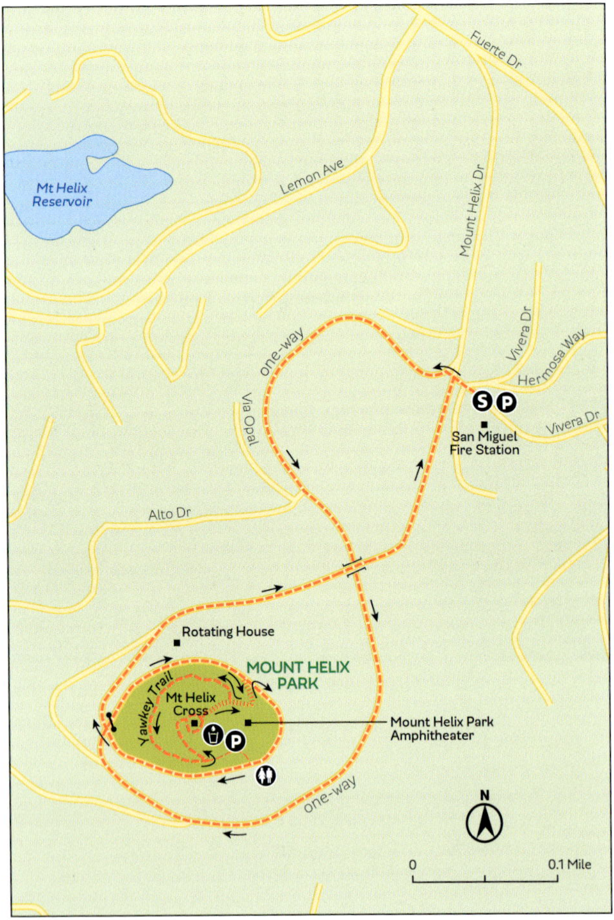

available in the large dirt lot on the left, across the street from the San Miguel Fire Station. For those with limited mobility or who are looking for a shorter stroll, there are also twelve spots at the top parking lot, as well as limited street parking in front of the office.

Named after a snail, the *Helix aspersa*, by Captain Rufus Porter in the nineteenth century, Mount Helix is known as the "Crown Jewel of East County." It is one of the most recognizable landmarks in San Diego, with a 35-foot-tall cross crowning the 1373-foot peak. The summit is located in Mount Helix Park, a free private park open to the public year-round. It was originally opened as a memorial to Mary Carpenter Yawkey in 1925 and was transferred to the Mount Helix Park Foundation in the 1990s.

With its panoramic views of San Diego, the Pacific Ocean, and the local mountains of South and East San Diego County, Mount Helix is a great place to watch the sunrise or sunset, enjoy a picnic, or take in a class or performance at its amphitheater. Though it is possible to drive close to the summit, this route maximizes exploration of the area by combining an uphill climb on pavement and the short dirt Yawkey Trail to create a 1.7-mile figure-eight loop.

GET MOVING

From the parking lot at the intersection of Vivera Drive and Mount Helix Drive, use the crosswalk to head northwest on Mount Helix Drive and begin walking uphill on the right side of the road. Mount Helix Drive is a one-way street that circles up and around the peak before returning downhill. For this route, follow the same direction as the one-way vehicle traffic. Take care, as there is no sidewalk. Throughout the hike, stay in the designated area for pedestrians, indicated by delineator posts, a safety berm, and a rugged, natural stone wall. This wall and the one surrounding the summit were built in 1933 by the Civil Works Administration. Since Mount Helix Park is surrounded by a developed neighborhood, take the opportunity to admire the architecture of the various houses and planted landscapes.

Shortly after you cross Alto Drive, move to the left-hand side of Mount Helix Drive to stay in the pedestrian area.

The Mount Helix amphitheater is popular for exercising and a great spot for community events.

Notice rocky outcrops and vegetation leading up to the peak on the right, as well as views of Mount San Miguel to the left. Continue straight on Mount Helix Drive, walking uphill through the gate for Mount Helix Park.

Enter the park to the right, using a staircase to climb to the signed junction of the Yawkey Trail. Turn right to follow the dirt trail as it winds around toward the summit. This hilltop is home to a wide variety of established native plants and wildlife, including insects, reptiles, birds, and mammals. Keep your eyes peeled for black sage, California live oak, California sagebrush, wild San Diego sweetpea, California sunflower, and lemonade berry. There are plant identification signs throughout the park with QR codes for more information, as well as interpretive panels pointing out landmarks.

At the end of the Yawkey Trail, turn left and follow the paved road up to the summit. Circle around the cross before turning right into the amphitheater. Here you will find many people taking advantage of the sprawling stairs for their fitness routines. Descend the stairs to the bottom of the amphitheater and turn left at the junction of the Yawkey Trail. Take the stairs back down to Mount Helix Drive and turn right.

Follow the road uphill as it loops around the peak, passing the office and restrooms. Move to the left side of the road to stay in the pedestrian area. Once you have passed the summit, cruise downhill. Cross the street past your uphill route and continue straight. Look to your right to catch one of the most unique dwellings in San Diego: the Rotating House. A full rotation of this house takes between thirty-three minutes to twenty-four hours, depending on what the homeowner prefers; it can even rotate in either direction. Cross to the right shoulder of the road and follow the pedestrian path back to the parking lot.

43 Dictionary Hill

DISTANCE: 2.2 miles roundtrip
ELEVATION GAIN: 500 feet
HIGH POINT: 1060 feet
DIFFICULTY: Moderate
FITNESS: Hikers, runners, and cyclists
FAMILY-FRIENDLY: Yes
DOG-FRIENDLY: Yes, leashed
BIKE-FRIENDLY: Yes
AMENITIES: None
CONTACT: County of San Diego
GPS: 32.72679°, –116.98345°

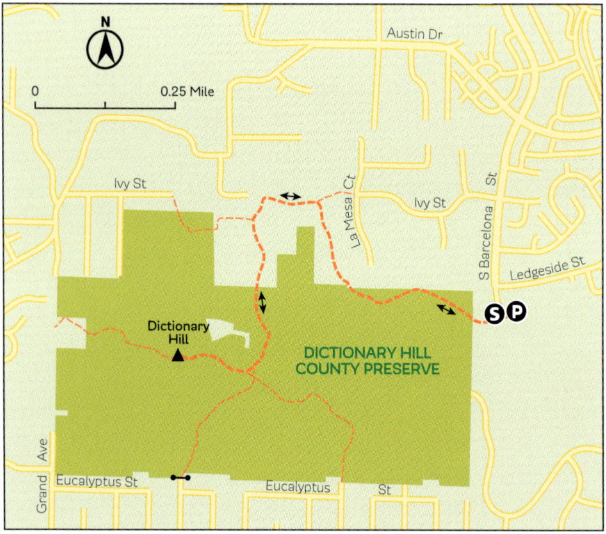

GETTING THERE

Map to: Dictionary Hill County Preserve

Public Transit: Take MTS Bus Route 855 to Sweetwater Springs Boulevard and Austin Drive. Head west along Austin Drive for about 0.7 mile, then turn left at South Barcelona Street and continue about 0.3 mile to the trailhead.

Parking: The trailhead is located at the end of South Barcelona Street, and parking can be found along the street.

Dictionary Hill County Preserve was created in 2018 and spans 175 acres of coastal sage scrub and chaparral habitat. This small hill provides a sweeping view of the South Bay from its summit.

GET MOVING

Starting from the trailhead at South Barcelona Street, walk through a thick grove of eucalyptus trees. Follow the trail to

To the summit of Dictionary Hill

the right along Bancroft Creek. You should see a sign pointing toward the summit of Dictionary Hill. Make a short climb, leaving the eucalyptus trees behind and transitioning into coastal scrub and chaparral. If it has rained, the creek may be flowing, but usually it is dry. After about 0.25 mile, look for a use-trail leading up the slope to your left. Ignore it and continue hiking to the west.

Continue another 0.2 mile, following the creek until you reach a fork in the trail. Take the left fork to start the climb up to the summit. This portion is steep and a bit rocky, so take your time. After about 0.25 mile, the grade will ease, and you will probably see some of the ongoing plant rehabilitation that is underway. Reach a ridgeline, where you will be greeted with a nice view of the Sweetwater Reservoir and Mother Miguel Mountain to the south. Turn right to follow the trail upward. Cross over the service road to the water tank that sits on the hill; from here, the summit is just another 0.15 mile away, but getting there requires another 80 feet of climbing.

The summit of Dictionary Hill is a wide, flat area. The center is closed, due to it being a sensitive habitat. Head to the western portion of the summit for a great view of the Silver Strand, Point Loma, the Coronado Bridge, and even the Coronado Islands off the coast of Mexico. Looking off to the north, you should be able to see various peaks in Mission Trails. To the east, El Cajon Mountain and Cuyamaca Peak are visible when the skies are clear. When you are ready to leave, retrace your route down from the summit. There are some other trails that lead down, but their condition is not as nice.

OPPOSITE: *Elevated walkway on the Otay River Valley Trail (Trail 51)*

SOUTH BAY

44 Coronado Walkabout

DISTANCE:	5.7 miles roundtrip
ELEVATION GAIN:	Minimal
HIGH POINT:	30 feet
DIFFICULTY:	Easy to moderate
FITNESS:	Walkers, runners, and cyclists
FAMILY-FRIENDLY:	Yes
DOG-FRIENDLY:	Yes, leashed and on pavement; permitted off-leash only on Dog Beach (200 Ocean Blvd.)
BIKE-FRIENDLY:	Yes, but must dismount in marked areas on boardwalk and Orange Ave.
AMENITIES:	Restrooms, picnic tables, and water
CONTACT:	Port of San Diego, City of Coronado
GPS:	32.69081°, -117.16490°
BEFORE YOU GO:	Coronado is a popular resort town. Go on mornings or weekdays for fewer crowds.

GETTING THERE

Map to: Tidelands Park, 2000 Mullinex Dr., Coronado, CA 92118

Public Transit: Take MTS Bus Route 904 to Glorietta Boulevard and 3rd Street. Walk southwest on the paved path through Tidelands Park to the Bayshore Bikeway. Another option is to take the Coronado Ferry from downtown San Diego to Coronado Ferry Landing and start your journey there.

Parking: From State Route 75 (San Diego–Coronado Bridge), turn right onto Glorietta Boulevard. Turn right on Mullinex Drive and follow it to the large parking lot. Find free parking here.

Coronado is a popular resort destination just a few minutes from downtown San Diego. Coronado, Spanish for "crowned," is nicknamed the Crown City. It is a tied island, connected to the mainland by the Silver Strand and the San Diego–Coronado Bridge. Coronado has a proud military history and

Views of the San Diego–Coronado Bridge from the paved Bayshore Bikeway at Tidelands Park

presence, home to Naval Air Station North Island and Naval Amphibious Base Coronado.

There are miles of paths with ocean and bay views, ideal for runners, walkers, and cyclists. This 5.7-mile paved loop circles the bulk of Coronado—a perfect way to explore all the island has to offer, including spectacular views, a beautiful stretch of coastline, the historical Hotel del Coronado, and a charming downtown.

GET MOVING

From the parking area at Tidelands Park, walk toward the water and turn right to join the Bayshore Bikeway path. Immediately, there is a spectacular vista of the landmark San

The SS Monte Carlo *shipwreck is visible at extremely low tide.*

Diego–Coronado Bridge. The curved blue bridge is 2.1 miles long and five lanes wide, with a clearance of approximately 200 feet for large ships to pass underneath. After about 0.2 mile, follow the path underneath the bridge, offering a unique perspective of the tall, tapering, arched piers. Walk alongside the Coronado Municipal Golf Course, turning left as the trail approaches and moves parallel to Glorietta Boulevard.

When the sidewalk ends at 0.7 mile, use the crosswalk to cross Glorietta Boulevard. Turn left and continue for about a

mile. At the second intersection of Glorietta Boulevard and San Luis Rey Avenue, use the crosswalk to move to the other side of Glorietta Boulevard. Turn right to link back up with the Bayshore Bikeway path.

Follow the paved path as it curves along Glorietta Bay, a secluded, picturesque area of the greater San Diego Bay. At 2.3 miles, just past the public restrooms and Coronado City Hall, take the path to the right, toward the road. At the intersection of Avenida de las Arenas and SR 75 (Silver Strand Boulevard), use the crosswalk to cross the street. Follow Avenida de las Arenas west through the public parking lot, then use the ramp up to Coronado Beach. This wide, sandy beach is 1.9 miles long, bordered by the US naval base beaches. It is routinely ranked as one of the nation's best beaches.

During the winter, you might want to explore the shoreline to the south. Here, the shipwreck of SS *Monte Carlo*, a gambling ship and former concrete hulled freighter that wrecked on New Year's Day 1931, is sometimes visible during extremely low tides. Otherwise, turn right and follow the pavement north, or use the stairs to walk on the beach.

At 2.9 miles, pass the iconic Hotel del Coronado, built in 1888 and a National Historic Landmark. It has also been the setting for movies, including Marilyn Monroe's *Some Like It Hot*. Turn left to follow the sidewalk sandwiched between the Pacific Ocean and Ocean Boulevard. There are great views of the coastline and the Point Loma peninsula, and you might notice sand dunes topped with ice plant. From an aerial view, these dunes are shaped to spell out the word *Coronado*.

Just past the lifeguard tower and restrooms at Isabella Avenue and Ocean Boulevard, use the crosswalk to cross the street. Follow Isabella Avenue for about a quarter mile before turning left on Orange Avenue, Coronado's dining and shopping hub, where the median of the street was once lined with orange trees. This is a great place to take a break or explore the downtown area. Follow Orange Avenue for about a mile. At the intersection of Orange Avenue and 1st Street, use the crosswalk to turn right on 1st Street, then make an immediate left onto the paved pathway to enter Centennial Park, with its amazing views of the San Diego skyline. It is also the site of the old San Diego Bay Ferry, used before the San Diego–Coronado Bridge was built in 1969. A historic ferry tollbooth still sits within this park. At the end of the park walkway, turn right to follow the bayside path.

At around 5 miles, pass through Coronado Ferry Landing Park, which has restrooms and restaurants. Follow the Bayshore Bikeway back to the start at Tidelands Park.

GO FARTHER

Continue on the 24-mile-long Bayshore Bikeway. Visit Star Park and the home that was rented out by author L. Frank Baum (at 1101 Star Park Circle) when he wrote three books in his Oz series.

45 Silver Strand State Beach

DISTANCE: 3.1 miles roundtrip
ELEVATION GAIN: Minimal
HIGH POINT: 20 feet
DIFFICULTY: Easy
FITNESS: Walkers and runners
FAMILY-FRIENDLY: Yes
DOG-FRIENDLY: No; allowed only in parking lots and RV campground
BIKE-FRIENDLY: Yes, but prohibited on unpaved trails and non-public access roads; must be walked through tunnels under State Route 75
AMENITIES: Restrooms, benches, picnic tables, showers, water, and a campground
CONTACT: California State Parks
GPS: 32.62431°, –117.13892°
BEFORE YOU GO: If you plan to swim, be aware that the ocean shoreline and bay are intermittently closed to public water contact when there is a threat to public health. Any closures will be posted.

GETTING THERE

Map to: 1568 Attu Ave., Coronado, CA 92118

Public Transit: Take MTS Bus Route 901 to SR 75 (Silver Strand Boulevard) and Attu Avenue. Walk south on SR 75

Mexico's Coronado Islands are visible from Silver Strand State Beach.

(Silver Strand Boulevard) and turn left on Attu Avenue to reach the trailhead.

Parking: From SR 75 (Silver Strand Boulevard), turn right onto Attu Avenue. There is limited free parking on the dirt shoulder of the street at the trailhead, on the bayside section of the park. Additional paid parking is available in the four large lots on the ocean side of Silver Strand State Beach at 5000 State Route 75, Coronado, CA 92118. The entrance gates to the beach open at 7 AM and close at 7 PM in the winter, 8 PM in the spring and fall, and 9 PM in the summer.

Silver Strand State Beach encompasses both the San Diego Bay and Pacific Ocean sides of the strand, a 7-mile sand spit connecting Coronado with Imperial Beach. Named for the delicate tracery of tiny silvery seashells lining its white sands, the strand offers stunning views of both the gentle San Diego Bay and the more turbulent ocean surf. The ocean side of the park features 2.5 miles of coastline with views of Point Loma and the Coronado Islands of Mexico, while the bay side is a

pedestrian-only area with a small network of trails in a coastal strand habitat. Silver Strand is off the beaten path, making it the perfect beach for those who want to avoid large crowds and enjoy peace and solitude.

GET MOVING

Walk through the white gate on Attu Avenue and take the trail to the left. Follow it alongside residential buildings for 0.2 mile to a rusty fence on the left and San Diego Bay in front of you. Take in the view of the bay and Coronado Bridge, then turn right on the trail. Continue on the sandy trail, peppered with seashells, as it parallels the bay. Though the coastal strand habitat is characterized by bare, wind- and spray-whipped sand, it is home to a fragile ecosystem that includes rare plants and ground-nesting birds. In the 1990s, much of the bay side was covered with thick mats of invasive sea fig, a succulent plant native to South Africa. After it was pulled in the early 2000s, a flora rich in sensitive plant species emerged, including the rare and seriously endangered Brand's phacelia,

currently found in just twelve locations worldwide (seven in the United States and five in Mexico).

At 0.4 mile, the trail curves west and becomes paved, hugging Crown Cove, an east-facing sandy beach on the bay.

Here, the water is calm and tends to be a little warmer than the ocean, ideal for sailing and swimming. At 0.7 mile, veer left at the trail junction and walk past the Crown Cove Aquatic Center and restrooms on the right. Continue until you reach 0.9 mile, then turn left onto the dirt trail running parallel to the paved path. Follow it for about a quarter of a mile until it merges back into the paved path, taking it to the right for a short distance before you reach a pedestrian tunnel. Use the tunnel to walk underneath SR 75, moving from the bay to the beach.

From the tunnel, walk through the parking lot, across the sand, and down to the shoreline. The beach here is very wide. When the current sweeps south past Point Loma, it deposits sand and sediment along the Silver Strand, so attention to tides is not necessary for this beach walk. Turn left and head south along the beach. Notice the Point Loma peninsula to the north and, to the south, the Imperial Beach Pier and the Coronado Islands of Mexico offshore. Watch for the western snowy plover, a federally endangered shorebird that nests in the Silver Strand Natural Preserve dunes.

Turn around at lifeguard tower zero at 1.8 miles. Retrace your steps along the beach, moving north. At 2.5 miles, just before the campground, turn right and cross the sand toward the picnic area. At the pavement, walk across the picnic area and parking lot to another pedestrian tunnel, crossing through and emerging on the bay side. Veer left to follow the pathway, and after a short distance, turn left onto the paved trail, continuing parallel to the Bayshore Bikeway to the left. At 2.8 miles, just past some picnic tables, turn left onto the dirt trail and follow it back to the starting point.

GO FARTHER

Silver Strand State Beach has connections to the 24-mile-long Bayshore Bikeway. Due to naval property on both sides of the beach, the only way to walk the entire length of the strand is to use the bike path that parallels SR 75.

46 Living Coast Discovery Center Trail

DISTANCE: 1 mile roundtrip
ELEVATION GAIN: Minimal
HIGH POINT: 15 feet
DIFFICULTY: Easy
FITNESS: Walkers
FAMILY-FRIENDLY: Yes
DOG-FRIENDLY: No
BIKE-FRIENDLY: No
AMENITIES: Restrooms and picnic tables
CONTACT: Living Coast Discovery Center
GPS: 32.63990°, −117.11100°
BEFORE YOU GO: Trail only accessible when Living Coast Discovery Center is open. Admission to discovery center not required to hike trail.

GETTING THERE

Map to: 1000 Gunpowder Point Dr., Chula Vista, CA 91910

Public Transit: Take the Blue Line Trolley to the E Street station, then walk north to E Street. Walk west under Interstate 5 to the traffic circle, then head northwest along Gunpowder Point Drive to the shuttle stop.

Parking: The free parking lot is located west of the corner of Bay Boulevard and E Street in Chula Vista. From Gunpowder Point Drive, take the first exit out of the traffic circle and turn left into the parking lot.

Note: This trail is next to the Living Coast Discovery Center in the San Diego Bay National Wildlife Refuge. Visitors cannot drive directly to the center, but must instead take the complimentary shuttle to the trailhead.

Living Coast Discovery Center is a small zoo and aquarium located on the San Diego Bay National Wildlife Refuge. Originally known as the Chula Vista Nature and Interpretive

Native Pollinator Garden at the Living Coast Discovery Center

Center, it is one of San Diego's hidden gems. While the discovery center charges an admission fee, the Native Pollinator Garden and Gunpowder Point Interpretive Trail do not.

GET MOVING

The shuttle will drop you off directly across from the Native Pollinator Garden. Take a moment to wander through the garden to learn more about pollinators. You can also see some of the ruins from when this area was used to produce gunpowder during World War I. Back in 1916, the Hercules Powder

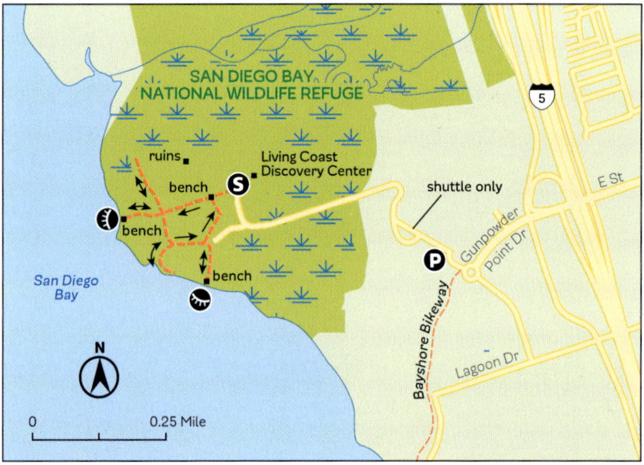

Company harvested giant kelp offshore and brought it here to be processed into gunpowder. With the end of World War I, the manufacturing plant was abandoned. When you are done exploring the garden, head south to the start of the Gunpowder Point Interpretive Trail.

This trail is unique, as it is best described as a hub-and-spoke route. Follow it west toward San Diego Bay. Along the way, find interpretive signs about the wildlife and history of the area. At 0.1 mile, reach the first junction and continue straight. If you need a break, several benches are conveniently located here. In another 0.1 mile, come to a four-way junction and follow the path to the right until it ends. Here you can view some of the ruins from the Hercules Powder Company, and there is a great view of the San Diego–Coronado Bridge and the San Diego skyline beyond.

After taking in the scene, return to the four-way junction and turn right toward the water. In just under 0.1 mile, reach the water's edge. You are not allowed to cross the ropes and enter the water, but two benches nearby allow you to soak in the views. Directly across the bay are the Silver Strand and the Coronado Cays.

Once again, return to that four-way junction and turn right, heading south. When the trail reaches a T intersection, take the path to the right, which will again end near the water's edge. Here you will find some mudflats, where you might find long-billed curlews, American avocets, red knots, long-billed dowitchers, or black-bellied plovers searching for food.

Return to the T intersection and head right. At the next junction, you should be able to spot a building and a nearby shade pavilion off to the southeast, which is the next stop. The trail now passes a small tidal pool before reaching a small, shaded pavilion. If you visit during the week, there is a good chance you will see schoolchildren along these trails.

When you are done enjoying the shade, return to the junction and continue straight. (The trail to the right at the junction leads to an employee-only area.) Follow the path as it heads northeast before turning north and returning to the first junction at the start of the hike. Walk back to the shuttle stop and either explore the Living Coast Discovery Center or wait for the shuttle to return you to the parking area.

GO FARTHER

Next to the parking area for the Living Coast Discovery Center is the Bayshore Bikeway, so you could walk or ride along it.

47 Rice and Snake Canyons Loop

DISTANCE: 4.3 miles roundtrip
ELEVATION GAIN: 260 feet
HIGH POINT: 450 feet
DIFFICULTY: Moderate
FITNESS: Hikers, runners, and cyclists
FAMILY-FRIENDLY: Yes

Snake Canyon Trail in Bonita

DOG-FRIENDLY:	Yes, leashed
BIKE-FRIENDLY:	Yes
AMENITIES:	Picnic tables; restrooms and water in Kumeyaay Park
CONTACT:	City of Chula Vista
GPS:	32.64477°, -117.01169°

GETTING THERE

Map to: Rice Canyon Demonstration Gardens

Public Transit: Take MTS Bus Route 709 to East H Street and Buena Vista Way. Walk north along Buena Vista Way for 0.5 mile, then right onto North Rancho del Rey Parkway. Rice Canyon Demonstration Gardens is on the left side of the street.

Parking: A small parking lot is available at the Rice Canyon Demonstration Gardens. Additional parking is available across the road in Kumeyaay Park.

Located in the city of Chula Vista, this loop passes through two different canyons, Rice and Snake. The Rice Canyon Trail is part of the California Riding and Hiking Trail (CRHT). For

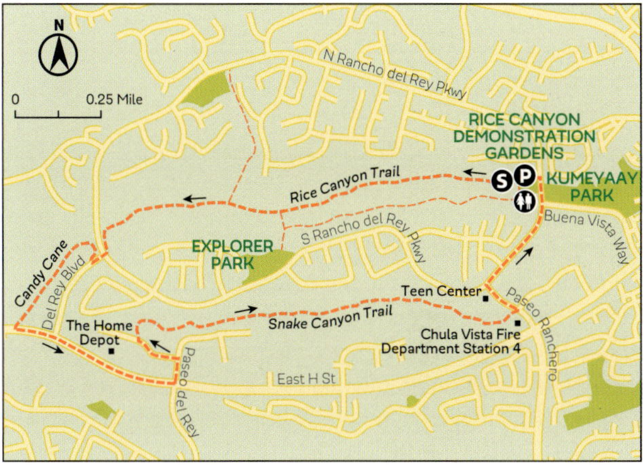

those unfamiliar with CRHT, it was to be a trail system that would have made a complete loop through the entire state of California. While a portion of the trail system was built, mostly in Southern California, various issues arose and efforts to complete this trail were halted. Snake Canyon, just to the south of Rice Canyon, is a popular mountain biking trail.

GET MOVING

From the west end of the demonstration gardens, find the kiosk and the start of the Rice Canyon Trail, a wide dirt path that heads west, passing through the canyon. Coastal chaparral lines the trail, and in the spring, wildflowers bloom. At regular intervals, CRHT trail markers—brown posts topped with yellow—line the sides of the trail. After 0.7 mile, a trail to the left connects to Explorer Park to the south, but you should continue straight.

At 1.4 miles, come to the intersection of North Rancho del Rey Parkway and del Rey Boulevard. Using the crosswalk, head across North Rancho del Rey onto Del Rey Boulevard to reach the next section, known as the Candy Cane.

If you look at a map for this upcoming trail segment, you will see that it does indeed resemble a candy cane. The path will hook around and continue for another 0.4 mile to East H Street.

Turn left onto East H Street and walk along the dirt trail for 0.1 mile to Del Rey Boulevard. Use the crosswalk to cross Del Rey Boulevard, then continue along the concrete sidewalk to East H Street. At 2.3 miles, turn left onto Paseo del Rey. Pass the gas station and follow the road into the parking lot. Find the trailhead into Snake Canyon near the northeast side of The Home Depot. The route weaves its way east through the canyon on a singletrack trail. The Snake Canyon Trail is favored by local mountain bikers because it has been enhanced on the turns. In fact, the bridges that were installed to cross the seasonal stream were sponsored by the San Diego Mountain Bike Association. Please keep an eye and ear open for riders along this section of the trail.

At 3.9 miles, the trail ends at Paseo Ranchero and Chula Vista Fire Department Station 4. Turn left and walk northwest along Paseo Ranchero until it dead-ends into South Rancho del Rey Parkway. After crossing South Rancho del Rey at the crosswalk, turn right and follow the sidewalk for 0.3 mile back to the demonstration gardens.

48 Sweetwater River Trail

DISTANCE: 3.7 miles roundtrip
ELEVATION GAIN: 350 feet
HIGH POINT: 280 feet
DIFFICULTY: Easy to moderate
FITNESS: Hikers, runners, and cyclists
FAMILY-FRIENDLY: Yes
DOG-FRIENDLY: Yes, leashed

Morrison Pond along the Sweetwater River Trail is great for bird-watching.

BIKE-FRIENDLY: Yes
AMENITIES: Restrooms and water
CONTACT: County of San Diego
GPS: 32.68335°, −117.00306°
BEFORE YOU GO: Trails open daily, dawn to dusk

GETTING THERE

Map to: Sweetwater Summit Regional Park

Public Transit: None

Parking: There is day-use parking to the left of the entrance station.

Starting from the Sweetwater Summit Regional Park, this trail begins with views of San Diego Bay and the Pacific Ocean to the west, before leading down into the Bonita Valley. Once on the valley floor, the trail follows the Sweetwater River—one of the five rivers in the County of San Diego—to Morrison

Pond. This pond is considered a birding hot spot, so take some time to see what you might discover.

GET MOVING

Find the Sweetwater Park trailhead just northwest of the entrance station. The trail leaves the mesa and descends about 0.3 mile toward a bridge spanning State Route 125 (the South Bay Expressway). This 264-foot bridge is named for Mary Augustine, who was instrumental in creating miles of horse and hiking trails through the Bonita Valley. A plaque in her honor is located on the west side of the bridge. Continue straight, as the trail to the left connects to the nearby baseball fields. A bench with a nice view of the Sweetwater River valley is placed at the switchback, so if you need a breather when returning up this switchback, this is a good place to stop.

Cross Conduit Road, passing horse stables and then following the edge of the Bonita Golf Course. This trail is popular with horseback riders, so be mindful of them, as they have the right-of-way along the trail. Step aside to let them pass, and make sure that if you have a dog with you, they are under control. After 0.7 mile, reach the end of the golf course and pass under Bonita Road. A pedestrian bridge crosses the river under the road above and leads to the north, but instead, continue walking westward.

In about 0.1 mile, come to the junction with the Blue Heron Trail. Follow this singletrack to your right, leaving the well-groomed trail behind. Here, you will hopefully see and hear more of the wildlife that inhabits this riparian environment. At 1.6 miles, the trail splits again, one fork going north and the other continuing west. The north fork crosses the river to the north side of Morrison Pond and another trailhead. If you decide to explore the north side, note that there is no bridge crossing the river, so you will have to get your feet wet if the water is flowing. Also, the trail does not directly loop around

the pond, so you will either need to backtrack to this junction or continue farther west before circumnavigating the pond.

For this route, because there are nice views of the pond from the south side, continue straight. This is a great location for bird-watching, so you may want to pack your binoculars for some closer views. When you are done enjoying the pond, continue along the trail as it arches southward and connects back with the Sweetwater Park Trail. Turn right and retrace your route. After making the climb back up to the trailhead, younger hikers might be rewarded with some time playing in the splash pad ($3 per person) near the trailhead.

GO FARTHER

Instead of heading west along the Sweetwater River, you can hike toward the east along the shores of the reservoir. For the very ambitious, link up with a trail that summits Mother Miguel Mountain to the east (Trail 49).

49 Mother Miguel Mountain

DISTANCE: 4.5 miles roundtrip
ELEVATION GAIN: 930 feet
HIGH POINT: 1520 feet
DIFFICULTY: Challenging
FITNESS: Hikers and runners
FAMILY-FRIENDLY: No
DOG-FRIENDLY: Yes, leashed
BIKE-FRIENDLY: No
AMENITIES: None; restrooms and water at Mount San Miguel Park
CONTACT: United States Fish and Wildlife Service, San Diego National Wildlife Refuge
GPS: 32.67235°, –116.97215°
BEFORE YOU GO: Trails open daily, dawn to dusk

GETTING THERE

Map to: Mother Miguel Mountain trailhead

Public Transit: Take MTS Bus Route 707 to Proctor Valley Road and Mount Miguel Road. Walk north along Mount Miguel Road for about 0.5 mile. Turn right onto Paseo Veracruz and after 0.3 mile, reach the trailhead.

Parking: You can either park along Paseo Veracruz or at Mount San Miguel Park. If you park along Paseo Veracruz, be mindful of the houses nearby.

Standing to the northeast of the trailhead is Mother Miguel Mountain (also known as Rock House), and behind it lies Mount San Miguel. These two peaks are often confused with one another. However, the latter is not accessible to the public. The summit of Mother Miguel offers sweeping views of southern San Diego and is a favorite for those living in the South Bay who are looking for a good workout.

The large rock cairn at the summit of Mother Miguel Mountain

GET MOVING

The trailhead is on the corner of Paseo Veracruz and Paseo los Gatos. Head out on the wide dirt path northward until it reaches a four-way junction. Do not take the trail that points straight north from the gate. This is not a sanctioned trail and is on San Diego Gas & Electric (SDGE) property. Instead, follow the wide road to your right—a service road for powerlines from the nearby San Miguel Substation—for about 0.5 mile until you reach the official trailhead.

After crossing a small ravine, come to a signboard with current trail information and other notices. The trail underwent a substantial redesign to combat massive erosion, and the scars from this misuse are still visible. Follow a series of

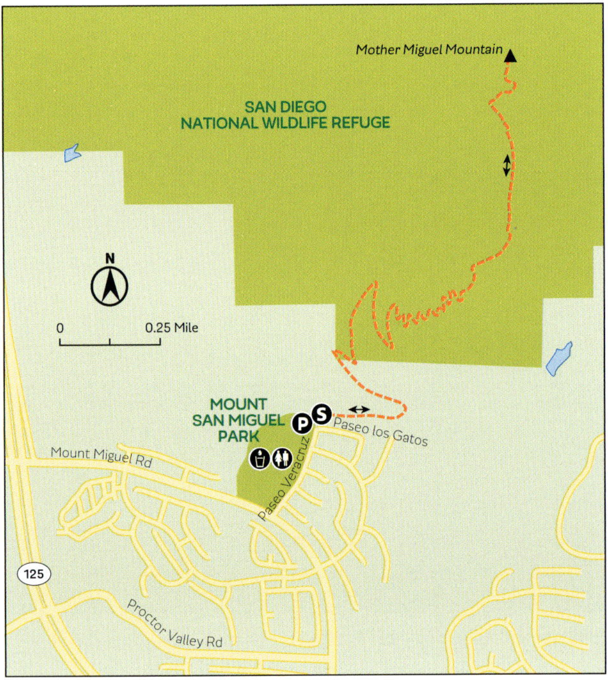

switchbacks as the new trail works its way upward (the old route went straight up the ridgeline).

As you climb, notice the Sweetwater Reservoir off to the north, with Otay Lakes visible to the south. To the east sits the now-closed Salt Creek Golf Course. After just over 1 mile, the switchbacks end and the trail's steepness eases as it turns more northward. Along your climb, California buckwheat, sagebrush, laurel sumac, and the occasional coastal barrel cactus line the slopes. Once at the summit, you are rewarded with sweeping views. There is a rock cairn that often sports a flagpole flying an American flag, as well as a POW and MIA flag. Once you have had your fill of the views of southern San Diego and Mexico, just retrace your route back down.

50 Otay Lakes Loop

DISTANCE: 1.5 miles roundtrip
ELEVATION GAIN: 420 feet
HIGH POINT: 800 feet
DIFFICULTY: Moderate
FITNESS: Hikers and runners
FAMILY-FRIENDLY: Yes
DOG-FRIENDLY: Yes, leashed
BIKE-FRIENDLY: No
AMENITIES: Restrooms, picnic area, and playground
CONTACT: County of San Diego
GPS: 32.60760°, -116.92923°
BEFORE YOU GO: Parking fee, payable at an entrance kiosk

GETTING THERE

Map to: Otay Lakes County Park
Public Transit: None
Parking: Follow Wueste Road past the Olympic Training Center to the end of the road at Otay Lakes County Park. Park along the east side of the park for the closest access to the trailhead.

Otay Lakes County Park covers 78 acres and is a great spot for bird-watchers. Located at the southern end of Lower Otay Lake, it offers a nice view of Savage Dam and the Otay River valley. This trail takes you past Camp Bashor, a joint venture with the County of San Diego and Scouting America (San Diego-Imperial Council), before making its way up to the park's highest point and rewarding you with a sweeping view of the area.

GET MOVING

This hike is a loop, so it can be done either clockwise or counterclockwise. We recommend doing it counterclockwise, as it affords a chance to warm up before tackling the climb to

Savage Dam and Otay Lakes from atop the park's highest point

the park's highest point, and it also offers views of the lake on your descent. From the east side of the park, you will see a sign for the trail that leads up the nearby hill—this will be the return path. Walk south along the paved road for a very short distance.

Notice the entrance to Camp Bashor, which is usually closed but offers family camping—check sdicscouting.org for availability and cost. The paved road turns to the right for additional parking. Instead, continue on the dirt road to your left. You will soon pass the camp's amphitheater, as well as the archery range. The trail continues south until it reaches a nice overlook of the Otay River. Unlike the wide river valley to the west, here the river passes through a rocky canyon.

The trail now begins its 0.5-mile climb to the summit. Stay on the switchbacks as you make your way up the slope. There will be connector trails leading to the north, linking back to

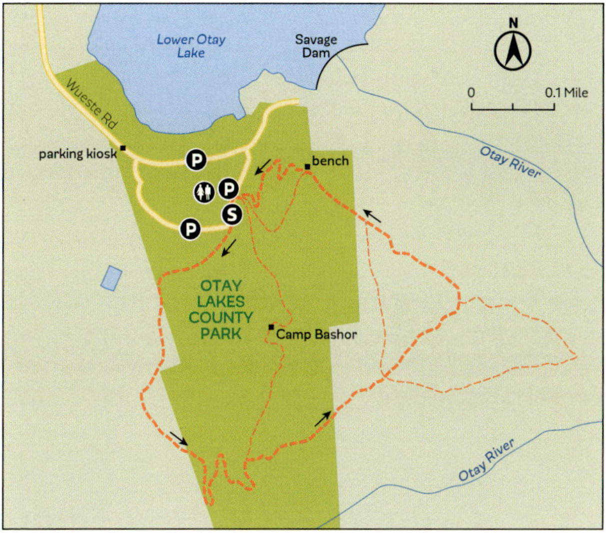

Camp Bashor, so if the climb becomes too difficult, you can use these to return to the start. Unfortunately, the switchbacks do end, and the route becomes a straight path to the summit, which makes it more challenging. Note that you may hear the sounds of gunfire because the San Diego Regional Firearms Training Center is located south of the park, across the river.

Come to a four-way junction just before you reach the summit. The trail to the right leads east and down to the Otay River, while the trail to the left bypasses the summit before connecting back to your return route. Continue straight for another 0.1 mile to the summit, and reward yourself with the views. Off to the east stands Otay Mountain.

When you are ready, head to the north and follow the trail down. Here you will have views of Lower Otay Lake and the Savage Dam. The trail is steep, so be mindful of your footing as you descend. After 0.2 mile from the summit, pass a concrete structure. Just past it is a nice bench where you can take a short break and enjoy the views to the north. You should spy the green grass of the park to the west, indicating that you have almost completed your loop. You can take either the service road or the trail to the west of the bench back down to complete the loop.

GO FARTHER

If you exit the park and walk along the road a short distance, you can take a side trail that follows the western shoreline of Lower Otay Lake. Since this lake is a drinking water reservoir, swimming is prohibited.

51 Otay River Valley Trail

DISTANCE: 4.7 miles roundtrip
ELEVATION GAIN: Minimal
HIGH POINT: 110 feet
DIFFICULTY: Easy
FITNESS: Walkers, hikers, runners, and cyclists
FAMILY-FRIENDLY: Yes
DOG-FRIENDLY: Yes, leashed
BIKE-FRIENDLY: Yes
AMENITIES: Restrooms and water
CONTACT: County of San Diego
GPS: 32.58808°, –117.07215°
BEFORE YOU GO: Mosquitoes are common here, so proper protection (bug spray or clothing) is recommended.

GETTING THERE

Map to: Otay Valley Regional Park Ranger Station

Public Transit: Take MTS Bus 934 to the Palm Avenue and Beyer Boulevard stop. Walk north on Beyer Boulevard for 0.3 mile to the ranger station.

Crossing over a portion of the Otay River

Parking: The ranger station and its parking lot are located on the west side of Beyer Boulevard. The parking lot has space for about seven cars.

Located just 4 miles north of the international border between the United States and Mexico, Otay Valley Regional Park (OVRP) is a multi-jurisdictional park managed by the County of San Diego, the City of Chula Vista, and the City of San Diego. OVRP offers more than 8 miles of trails along the Otay River for use by hikers, bicyclists, and equestrians. Along the river, several ponds allow for outstanding bird-watching opportunities.

GET MOVING

From the ranger station, head north to a kiosk to reach the primary east-west trail for OVRP. Turn right and cross Beyer Boulevard at the crosswalk. There is a low metal gate on the other side of the road, so cyclists or those pushing a stroller will have to lift their gear over this barrier. Follow the wide dirt

OTAY VALLEY REGIONAL PARK
805
5
to
eucalyptus trees
Finney Trail
Iglesia Ni Cristo
Palm Ave trailhead
Otay River
Finney Overlook
Myrtle S. Finney ES
Le May Pond
bench
Heart Pond
Fenton Pond
ranger station
Montgomery High School
Main St
Palm Ave
Hilltop Dr
Beyer Way
3rd Ave
4th Ave
Beyer Blvd
0
0.25 Mile
N

trail along the river valley and through the mix of coastal scrub riparian habitats that line it. At various points along the trail, interpretive signs in English and Spanish provide information about the plants, wildlife, and history of the region. In about 0.3 mile, come to Heart Pond. While you may not be able to see the heart-shaped outline of the pond from the ground, it is quite clear from above.

At 0.5 mile, reach a junction and take the left trail to continue. (The trail to the right leads to Beyer Way and one of the other seven trailheads for OVRP.) The path splits almost immediately—take the right trail to continue eastward.

Pass under Beyer Way and reach a T intersection. Take the trail to the right, following it for 0.1 mile to another junction. There, turn left to resume hiking eastward. In another 0.1 mile, the trail splits. One route climbs slightly up the valley slope, while the other remains along the valley floor. Take the valley floor option to reach Le May Pond, a short distance away. There is a nice bench located here—a good place to take a break or do some bird-watching. Just remember, it is illegal to feed the birds.

From Le May Pond, continue east 0.7 mile until you reach another junction. Stay straight here, heading east; you will return on the trail to the left. Off to your right, notice a trail climbing up the canyon wall to the mesa, which takes you up to Finney Overlook. This optional excursion adds another 0.6 mile to the hike and a climb of about 130 feet, but it does offer a wonderful view of the Otay River valley. Continue straight along the river for another 0.4 mile, following the trail as it makes a hard left turn, heading north toward a nice grove of eucalyptus trees. Interstate 805 will be just to the east. This grove is a nice spot for a break under the shade.

When you are ready to continue, take the singletrack trail to the left, due west. Work your way along the valley floor, and at 2.5 miles, reach a junction, taking the right fork toward the northwest. Soon, use a couple of small bridges to cross the Otay River before the trail turns left and resumes a more westerly direction.

Once you reach the Palm Avenue trailhead junction, follow the trail left, heading south and crossing the river one final time. At 3 miles, return to the junction for Finney Overlook that you passed earlier. From here, turn right, following the trail back to the ranger station where you started.

GO FARTHER

From the ranger station, the trail also continues west. Fenton Pond lies a mere 0.1 mile farther, with a trail that wraps almost all the way around it, affording more opportunities for bird-watching. Beyond the pond, the trail system continues west until it connects with the Bayshore Bikeway, where you can add on an additional 20-plus miles of hiking or riding opportunities.

52 Tijuana Estuary

DISTANCE:	4.3 miles roundtrip
ELEVATION GAIN:	Minimal
HIGH POINT:	20 feet
DIFFICULTY:	Easy
FITNESS:	Walkers, hikers, runners, and cyclists
FAMILY-FRIENDLY:	Yes
DOG-FRIENDLY:	Yes, leashed
BIKE-FRIENDLY:	Yes
AMENITIES:	Restrooms and water
CONTACT:	Tijuana River National Estuarine Research Reserve
GPS:	32.57483°, -117.12592°
BEFORE YOU GO:	Trails open daily, dawn to dusk

GETTING THERE

Map to: 301 Caspian Way, Imperial Beach, CA 91932

Tijuana Estuary is Southern California's largest coastal wetland.

Public Transit: Take MTS Bus Route 933 to Imperial Beach Boulevard and 3rd Street. Head south along 3rd Street. When it turns into Caspian Way, take the North McCoy Trail to the visitor center.

Parking: The visitor center is one block south of Imperial Beach Boulevard and three blocks from the ocean. A gravel parking lot is in front of the visitor center.

Tijuana River National Estuarine Research Reserve is Southern California's largest coastal wetland. This trail allows you to explore the northern portion of the reserve. Begin by stopping at the visitor center (no fee), where you can learn more about the reserve before heading out. Since the Tijuana Estuary supports 370 species of birds, including several endangered species, it is popular among bird-watchers. You can check out a pair of binoculars to help you view wildlife along the trail. The center keeps a list of recently confirmed sightings to help you identify the birds you might encounter.

Mar Vista High School
Imperial Beach Blvd
2nd St
3rd St
4th St
North McCoy Trail
Caspian Way
IMPERIAL BEACH SPORTS PARK
visitor center
Seacoast Dr
St
Ln
Fern Ave
5th St
California
Louden
Grove Ave
North McCoy Trail
Oneonta Ave
bench
bench
Iris Ave
South McCoy Trail
Visitor Center Trail
Pacific Ocean
Oneonta Slough
TIJUANA RIVER NATIONAL ESTUARINE RESEARCH RESERVE
Naval Outlying Landing Field Imperial Beach
River Mouth Loop
River Mouth Loop
bench
Tijuana River
N
0
0.25 Mile

GET MOVING

From the visitor center, head south about 500 feet and take the North McCoy Trail. This flat, wide trail crosses a finger of the Oneonta Slough (pronounced "sloo") and ends at 0.3 mile. Two benches offer places to rest and scan for any wildlife that might be here. Across the water, you can see the end of the South McCoy Trail, where you are heading next. Head back toward the visitor center, but at the Y junction, go right onto the River Mouth Trail. Initially, homes will be on your left and the estuary on your right.

At 1 mile, pass the Iris Avenue trailhead. It has space for three cars (one spot is for disabled parking) and can be used if you arrive before the main parking lot is open. As you continue, the homes are replaced with the Naval Outlying Landing Field. You may get to observe flying things of a different nature if the Navy is using this airfield. After about 200 feet, spot a trail to your right. This is your return trail. For now, continue another 0.2 mile to where the trail turns right (west). Directly to the south is the Tijuana River, which has a contamination problem, so we do not recommend hiking this portion after a rainstorm. Pass a junction with the South McCoy Trail, but continue straight. At the next junction, at about 2 miles, take a left to the overlook, where a bench awaits you for a break or some bird-watching. Often, you will see brown pelicans, curlews, and least terns (in summer).

When you are ready to continue, head back north and take the South McCoy Trail. At 2.7 miles, reach its end. Across the water, you should recognize the North McCoy Trail. Yet another bench is here for you to sit and enjoy the reserve. To return, retrace your route for about 0.5 mile to the previous junction, then take the left trail, which is a connector trail back to the River Mouth Trail. In 0.1 mile, turn left on the River Mouth Trail, and soon you will be back at the visitor center.

ACKNOWLEDGMENTS

To all the individuals I have had the opportunity to hike with over the years, I want to thank you for being the inspiration and foundation for *Urban Trails: San Diego*. Special thanks to Larry Kara, Christine Kara, Patrick Kara, Madelyn Kara, Ashley Kara, Kade Slater, Kyli Slater, Brianna Slater, Calista Slater, Gail Welch, Han Asoy, Matt Bennett, Greg Gerlach, Matt Hanan, Ted Markus, Jennifer Coady, Samantha Merz, Noel Norcross, Erika Lawson, Tara Kizer, Whitney Mann, Jackie Nematbakhsh, Monique Vargas, Noemi Portilla, and Sarah Moehlenbruck.

Special thank you to Larry Kara, Christine Kara, Gail Welch, and Kade Slater, who hiked routes and thoughtfully proofread my draft manuscripts. I am indebted to Erika Lawson, who not only hiked each and every one of my routes, but also provided helpful and meticulous feedback on my content and writing.

Thank you to the people at Mountaineers Books, especially Emily White, Laura Shauger, Callie Stoker-Graham, and Janet Kimball for patiently handling questions and providing feedback. Thank you to my coauthor, Chris Griffith, the drive behind making this book a reality.

Thank you to my family. Thank you to my husband, Kade Slater, for his enthusiasm, support, and willingness to let me spend most of my free time hiking and writing. Thank you to my parents, who have always been there for me and have provided unwavering support. Thank you to my brother, Patrick Kara, who gifted me my first pair of hiking boots and took me on my first hike (Santiago Peak, 15 miles with 4000 feet of elevation gain). Thank you to my girls—Kyli, Brianna, and Calista—for joining me on adventures. I am so grateful to have you all in my life.

—SUSIE KARA SLATER

There are several people that I want to thank for all their support during the process of writing this book. I may do a lot of solo hiking, but I am never alone on the trails.

First, to my lovely bride of thirty-plus years, Anita, who has been so incredibly supportive throughout all my hiking adventures over the years—thank you for reading and editing all those trip reports, and these trail guides, and listening to me blabber on and on about hikes, gear, and other related nonsense.

Thank you to my twins, Ben and Shira, for your patience as your dad went exploring on so many weekends.

To my sister, Mindy, you always loved following all my adventures virtually; you are dearly missed.

To my coauthor, Susie Kara Slater: from that first hike together in 2017, we have shared a lot of miles. You are truly a force of nature, and I am happy to have taken this journey of authorship together.

Thank you to Ted Markus, who routinely joins me on many of my adventures. I am sure you never quite understood what you were signing up for when you said, "Sure, I will go hiking with you . . ."

Thank you, Derek Loranger (a.k.a. 100Peaks), who knew what that challenge would spawn...

To my other principal hiking partners—Matt Bennet, Larry Edmonds, Greg Gerlach, Matt Hanan, Jeff Hester, David Lipsitz, and Gina Norte—I treasure all the miles spent together across those trails and summits.

Finally, a big thank you to the team at Mountaineers Books, especially Emily White, Laura Shauger, Callie Stoker-Graham, and Janet Kimball, for all the support and guidance in helping make this book a reality.

—CHRIS GRIFFITH

RESOURCES

MANAGING AGENCIES

California State Parks
www.parks.ca.gov

City of Chula Vista
www.chulavistaca.gov

City of Coronado
www.coronado.ca.us

City of La Mesa
www.cityoflamesa.us

City of San Diego
www.sandiego.gov

County of San Diego
www.sdparks.org

Living Coast Discovery Center
www.thelivingcoast.org

Mission Trails Regional Park Foundation
www.mtrp.org

Mount Helix Park Foundation
www.mthelixpark.org

National Park Service
www.nps.gov

Port of San Diego
www.portofsandiego.org

San Diego State University Mission Valley
www.missionvalley.sdsu.edu

Tijuana River National Estuarine Research Reserve
www.trnerr.org

US Fish and Wildlife Service
www.fws.gov

LOCAL ORGANIZATIONS

Balboa Park
www.balboapark.org

Cabrillo National Monument Foundation
www.cnmf.org

California Native Plant Society, San Diego Chapter
www.cnpssd.org

Canyoneers of the San Diego Natural History Museum
www.sdnat.org/canyoneers

Circulate San Diego
www.circulatesd.org

Dictionary Hill Open Space Advocates
www.dictionaryhill.info

Earth Discovery Institute
www.earthdiscovery.org

Friends of Coast Walk Trail
www.friendsofcoastwalk.org

Friends of Famosa Slough
www.famosaslough.org

Friends of Los Peñasquitos Canyon Preserve
www.penasquitos.org

Friends of Rose Canyon
www.rosecanyon.org

Friends of San Diego Wildlife Refuges
www.friendsofsdrefuges.org

Friends of Tecolote Canyon
www.friendsoftecolotecanyon.org

Groundwork San Diego–Chollas Creek
www.groundworksandiego.org

Hiking Meetups
www.hiking.meetup.com

I Love a Clean San Diego
www.cleansd.org

Kumeyaay Information
www.kumeyaay.info/kumeyaay

Liberty Station
www.libertystation.com

MAKE Projects
www.sdmake.org

San Diego Canyonlands
www.sdcanyonlands.org

Sierra Club, San Diego Chapter
www.sandiegosierraclub.org

Torrey Pines Conservancy
www.torreypines.org

Urban Corps of San Diego County
www.urbancorpssd.org

INDEX

ABOUT THE AUTHORS

KIM BISHOP

Born and raised in San Diego, **Susie Kara Slater** hikes more than two thousand miles per year, navigating the desert, mountains, snow-covered peaks, and more—with and without established trails. Her knowledge of hiking in the area is current and expansive. She was the first-ever finisher of the San Diego 100 Peaks Challenge in 2017; she also completed the San Diego Sierra Club County Peaks list in 2020. Off the trail, Susie is a pediatric occupational therapist and yoga instructor. She enjoys spending time with her family and her dog, Gizmo, exploring near and far; she is an avid world traveler of more than one hundred countries. This is her first book. Visit her on Instagram @susiehikes.

Chris Griffith is a California native and a graduate of the University of California, Santa Barbara, who is pursuing a graduate degree in outdoor recreation economy from the University of Colorado, Boulder. After becoming a British Canoe Union 3-star paddler, he switched his focus to hiking. In 2019, he became the third finisher of the 100 Peaks Challenge, which consisted of summiting one hundred peaks in San Diego County in a calendar year. Since then, he has completed the San Diego Sierra Club County Peaks list, numerous Six Pack of Peaks Challenges (SoCal, San Diego, Central Coast, and Arizona Winter), and the yearly Coast to Crest Challenge.

BEN GRIFFITH

Beyond hiking, Chris has a deep passion for spaceflight (american-spacecraft.org) and the history of the atomic age (atomicarchive.com). When not out hiking or backpacking, he can be found at home with his wife, Anita, and their dog, Rocky. Visit him online at sdpeakbagger.com or on Instagram @sdpeakbagger.

MOUNTAINEERS BOOKS

SKIPSTONE BRAIDED RIVER

recreation • lifestyle • conservation

MOUNTAINEERS BOOKS, including its two imprints, Skipstone and Braided River, is a leading publisher of quality outdoor recreation, sustainability, and conservation titles. As a 501(c)(3) nonprofit, we are committed to supporting the environmental and educational goals of our organization by providing expert information on human-powered adventure, sustainable practices at home and on the trail, and preservation of wilderness.

Our publications are made possible through the generosity of donors, and through sales of more than 700 titles on outdoor recreation, sustainable lifestyle, and conservation. To donate, purchase books, or learn more, visit us online:

MOUNTAINEERS BOOKS
1001 SW Klickitat Way, Suite 201 · Seattle, WA 98134
800-553-4453 · mbooks@mountaineersbooks.org
www.mountaineersbooks.org

An independent nonprofit publisher since 1960

YOU MAY ALSO LIKE:

LEAVE NO TRACE

Mountaineers Books is proud to support the Leave No Trace Center for Outdoor Ethics, whose mission is to use the power of science, education, and stewardship to ensure a sustainable future for the outdoors and the planet. The Leave No Trace program is focused specifically on human-powered (nonmotorized) recreation. For more information, visit www.lnt.org.